Understanding
Calculator
Math

Getting together the basic information, formulas,
facts, and mathematical tools you need to "unlock"
the real power of your *Handheld Calculator* —
at home — on the job — in school or college —
throughout your everyday life.

Note: The calculator keystrokes and descriptions
used in this book are applicable to many calculators
made by several manufacturers. The facts and
information included will be useful when working
any calculator, but the keystroke sequences
may vary slightly.

Radio Shack®

A DIVISION OF TANDY CORPORATION
FT. WORTH, TEXAS 76102

This book was developed by:

The Staff of the
Texas Instruments Learning Center
P. O. Box 225012, MS-54, Dallas, Texas 75265

Ralph A. Oliva Ph.D., Educational Software Director
M. Dean LaMont
Linda R. Fowler

with contributions by:

Elizabeth McIntosh
Joe Poyner
Jerry Moore
Joe Prock
Alecia S. Helton
David Clemens
Jacquelyn F. Quiram

in cooperation with:

The Staff of the University of
Denver Mathematics Laboratory

Dr. Ruth I. Hoffman, Director
Michael R. Zastrocky
Richard Reeser
Lucille P. Grogan

Artwork and layout were coordinated and executed by:

Barbara Beasley
Schenck, Plunk and Deason

IMPORTANT

ISBN 0-89512-016-X
Library of Congress Catalog Number: 78-50808

Table of Contents

Introduction

This book is designed for you. Its main purpose is to get together in one place a wide variety of useful and interesting information involving calculators, the world around you, and mathematics. It's designed to be a working tool that, when used with your calculator, becomes a system for problem solving as well as a key to discovery. We hope you'll have fun reading and exploring with it.

The Story of Mathematics

It is said that mathematics began long ago in Early Egypt. The Nile River would flood on occasion and wash away all landmarks and monuments. People needed a way to know where their land was after these floods, so methods of earth measurement (later to be called Geometry) were invented. The Greeks, always thinking, picked up those techniques, developed them further, and added new ideas such as Algebra and Trigonometry. Math was off and running. It was used in oceanic exploration. It was interesting. It was fun. Mathematics was used to help learn about the ways in which the world worked, what it looked like, and how much things cost. Calculus, statistics, and income taxes were invented.

The Story of Calculators

As mathematics began to grow, people started to notice that there were some parts of it that were not nearly as much fun as others. Downright tedious, in fact. Getting answers not only involved looking carefully at nature and people and analyzing them (fun part), but also often involved adding, subtracting, multiplying and dividing very cumbersome numbers (not so much fun part). People began looking for tools to help them handle the arithmetic part of mathematics more easily.

First, stones were used for counting things and keeping track. Then these were placed on a lined table or strung on a frame to form the abacus (a device still widely used in many parts of the world). Calculating tools then evolved — somewhat slowly — and a series of mechanical devices developed starting in

the 1600's with ideas from men such as John Napier. The first
real calculating machine was invented by a Frenchman named
Blaise Pascal — for handling monetary transactions. It was a
complex entanglement of gears, wheels and windows. Next came
even more complex whirling and whizzing mechanical units, with
buttons, wheels and hand cranks. Bigger machines using relays
and punched cards came about as electricity was applied to mathematics in helping take the 1890 U.S. Census.

Computers were born and began to grow. Sliderules (easy to use
and much more accessible than computers) were invented to help
take some of the tedium out of long calculations.

The Electronic Handheld Calculator

Then, a few years ago, people working in electronics began making
some breakthroughs that resulted in the inexpensive, accurate
and reliable handheld calculator. Calculator Math became
available to everyone. Now, throughout the world, people are
finding these little devices to be powerful allies as they
handle numbers and math in their everyday lives.

Math is all around us and is part of many daily activities.
Your calculator allows you to handle many of these problems
quickly and accurately — without having to hassle with lengthy,

tedious computations. This book has been designed to show you how. What we've tried to do is put together an accessible and compact package of the principles you need to take your problems and easily work them with keyboard solutions. This book was designed to work together with your calculator — to open up all its secrets and let you have more complete access to its power. Use them together! Both of them have been designed for you.

Experiment! Find how many heartbeats in a lifetime. How many Saturday nights are there until you're 85? What's the best buy? What's your correct change?

The first step is to really get acquainted with your calculator — to put it through its paces and see all aspects of how it operates. Chapter I of this book is a quick "tour" of the features and keys on most calculators, along with a brief look at *why* each key or feature is there, as well as *how* each can be useful. This "tour" is important — it will familiarize you with the scope and power of your machine. The subsequent chapters are packed with approaches to common mathematical problems in a variety of fields and the details you'll need in putting together quick, accurate solutions on your calculator. Along the way you'll find some bits of history or challenging ideas that may take you beyond a specific problem into further explorations with numbers.

Remember, too, that although your calculator is packed with the latest in state-of-the-art solid state technology, it needs love and respect, as well as occasional use as a toy. Don't be afraid to play with it — it's rugged and durable enough to be used anywhere. You may find yourself exploring patterns and relationships which can lead you to a whole new appreciation of the beautiful side of numbers and mathematics.

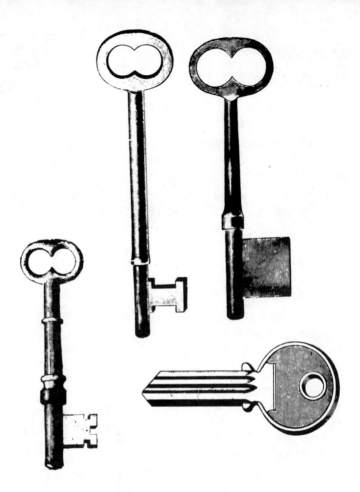

Note: The keys and features described in this section and used throughout this book are common to many calculators made by several manufacturers.

For simplicity, the key symbols used are taken from the TI-30 calculator. They may be slightly different from the keys on your calculator—your owners manual should clarify which keys perform each function.

The keystroke sequences shown assume your calculator has at least one memory, two levels of parentheses and scientific notation.

Answers may vary slightly in the final decimal place since each calculator has its own technique for rounding the answer.

When in doubt about what your calculator does, check your owner's manual.

BASIC KEYS
Introduction

Today's handheld calculators are rugged and inexpensive enough to be a natural and go anywhere "tool" for helping to handle the side of your life that involves numbers and mathematics. Your calculator can help in exploring and learning about mathematics itself, as well as in solving a variety of number problems from everyday living. They are a *natural* part of living today — a technological answer to the real need we all have for quick, accurate calculations. Any calculator, however, is "no more functional than the knowledge of the person who operates it". As with any convenience or tool, whether it's a pen, wrench, car, radio or whatever, it's important to get the "feel" of it. Check out all of its features — get familiar with what it will (and will not) do for you.

To better help you get acquainted, this chapter is a quick tour of the essential features and keys of most calculators. Some information is included on *why* each key is important, as well as *how* each works. After completing this tour, you'll be better able to use your calculator to unlock the world of mathematics — whether tallying your grocery bill or exploring the behavior of some new function or concept you haven't seen before. Above all — have fun with your calculator! We hope "Understanding Calculator Math" will provide some new ways for you to look at an important side of your life.

Battery Installation/ Considerations

If your calculator is of the TI-30 type, it operates on a standard 9-volt (non-rechargeable) battery. For best results it's recommended that you use an *ALKALINE* battery in your calculator. If you use a non-alkaline battery, it's important to remove it before storing your calculator or at the first signs of discharge. (If you don't — there's danger of damage to the unit from battery leakage.) It's time for a new battery at the *first* signs of erratic display or calculating behavior, and replacing the battery right away is always the best practice.

To install a battery in a TI-30, just insert a small coin into the slot on the back of the calculator case, and pry up the cover gently. Be careful not to tug on the battery wires when handling the snap connectors on the battery. When your new battery's connected, slide the ridged edge of the cover into the case and snap down the edge with the little latch. That's all there is to it!

Check your owner's manual for instructions on replacing batteries and recharging your calculator.

BASIC KEYS
ON/C Key — Turn It On/Clearing

The ON key on the calculator keyboard (or ON/OFF switch) turns the calculator on (power "on" is indicated by lighted digits in the display). Just turning most calculators on from the "off" condition clears everything inside to zero, and a **0.** should appear in the display.

Machines vary as to the keys used for clearing them. (Clearing is basically the process of sweeping any previous calculations from your machine in preparation for new ones.) With TI-30 type calculators the **ON/C** key is also used as a clear key. Others may have different arrangements — check your owner's manual.

● *ONE push of the CLEAR key clears the last number you entered into the calculator,* as long as the number wasn't followed by a function or operation key. (So if you hit a 5 instead of a 6 in the middle of a problem, just hit **ON/C** once, and try again.)

● If the CLEAR key is pushed right after an operation or function key (including the **=** key), the display, constant and all operations are cleared.

● *TWO pushes of the CLEAR key clears the entire calculator,* except for what's in memory. (The memory is a storage place for numbers you need to use over and over — we'll say more about it later on.)

● Check your owner's manual for the differences between a *clear* key and a *CLEAR ENTRY* or *CLEAR DISPLAY* key.

BASIC KEYS
The Display

To check out your calculator's display, turn it on and then push the ⎡ 8 ⎤ key until the display is filled with 8's. (In the TI-30 there should be 8* of them, and check to be sure that all of the parts of all your 8's are lit up.) You can enter up to eight* digits into the calculator at any one time; digit keys pressed after the 8th* key are ignored. (Internally, however, a calculator may work with more digits than shown in the display – see "Data Entry" section.)

Now press the CLEAR key twice and press the decimal point key ⎡ · ⎤ and the change sign key ⎡+/–⎤ . The change sign key changes the sign of any displayed number, and allows you to enter *negative numbers* – those numbers *less than zero* that we all have to deal with from time to time (such as money owed, etc.).

Your calculator's display really has a powerful bundle of technology behind it. If your display is made up of small, bright red digits, each segment is a little diode made of Gallium arsenide (GaAs), a substance which emits light when electric current is passed through it under just the right conditions. If your display is bright green, your digits are of the *vacuum fluorescent* (VF) variety, where a gas discharge provides the light for the display segments. If your display is made up of darker digits on a silver or silver/green background it's of the *liquid crystal* variety. Liquid Crystal Displays (LCD's) use an electro-chemical action to change the physical appearance of the display digits, and use very little electric power.

Each number you see in your display isn't lit up or activated all at once either. All the display segments are turned on and off very rapidly ("strobed") by the electronic "brain" of your calculator, so fast that your eye puts the segments together into numbers. (Shake your calculator slightly while watching the display, and you'll begin to catch the display in the act.) Once the number is lit up, specially designed lens systems and colored windows are often used to get the light to you as a clean, easy to read display.

*these vary from calculator to calculator, so check your owner's manual for specifics.

BASIC KEYS
OFF — Key and
POWER SAVER!!

The OFF key or ON/OFF switch just turns off the calculator, plain and simple. Turning the calculator off and on will clear most calculators completely — including the memory.

TI-30 type calculators have an added bonus feature — automatic shutoff power saving circuitry. If you leave the calculator on without activating any keys, the calculator takes these steps to save power:

1) After typically 25 to 30 seconds the display (which consumes the most power) shuts down to a single traveling decimal point which moves across the display from left to right. As soon as any key is depressed the display comes "back to life". (A good way to reactivate the display is to press the EXC key twice. This makes sure that any calculations in progress or data in the machine are all unaffected.)

2) If the calculator continues in the traveling decimal mode uninterrupted for 7 to 14 minutes, it quietly shuts itself off!

Working together these two features can save up to 50% on battery life. The common problem of inadvertently leaving your calculator on when not in use is solved! To see if your calculator has a power saving feature, refer to your owner's manual.

BASIC KEYS

| 0 | - | 9 | | . | | +/- | —

Data Entry Keys

Most of today's calculators provide a full floating decimal point, and numbers are entered into the machine with the data entry keys: [0] - [9] [.] [+/-] . As you press number keys, the decimal point remains to the right of your entry until the decimal point key [.] is pressed. The fractional part of the number is then keyed in and the decimal point floats to the left with it. To change the sign of a number in the display just push the change sign key [+/-] once. (Pressing [+/-] again changes the sign back again).

ACCURACY:

With most calculators you can directly enter numbers up to 8 digits in length. Your calculator may hold and work internally with more digits*— for extra accuracy. In these cases, you can enter numbers with more digits than appear in the display as the sum of two numbers, as shown below. (As an example, results of calculations are computed to eleven digits in the TI-30, and then rounded off to 8 digits in the display).

Example: To enter the maximum number of digits, for instance, an eleven-digit number — 418413.23106.

Press	**Display/Comments**
418413 [+]	**418413.** The whole part of the number.
.23106 [=]	**418413.23**

*these numbers vary from calculator to calculator, so check your owner's manual for specifics.

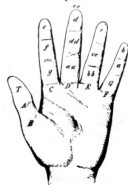

BASIC KEYS

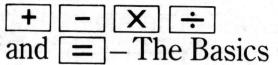

and ⊟ – The Basics

If you're looking at buying a new car, there are certain basic things you must have before you start checking out the extra options. Calculators have "basics", too – the four basic operations.

When you press the ⊟ key, all pending operations (things waiting to happen inside the calculator) are completed, you get your result, and the calculator is cleared – ready to start on the next problem. Here are a couple of quick examples:

⊞ ⊟

You start with $150 in your checking account, and write checks for $10, $45.25, $15, and then make a $50 deposit; what's your balance?

Press   **Display/Comments**

150 ⊟ 10 ⊟ 45.25
⊟ 15 ⊞ 50 ⊟   **129.75**   Your balance.

⊠ ⊞ : If pencils cost $6.48 per gross, how much will 47 of them cost? (A "gross" of anything is 144 of them.)

Press   **Display/Comments**

6.48 ⊞ 144 ⊠ $6.48 ⊞ 144 is how much
                       1 pencil costs
47 ⊟   **2.115**   Cost of 47 pencils
                       (You'd probably pay $2.12.)

BASIC KEYS
AOS™– The Algebraic Operating System

Mathematics is a science which is persnickety about some things. One of them is that it never permits two different answers to the same series of computations. Because of this requirement – one solution for any computation – mathematicians have established a set of accepted (and universal) rules when mixed operations are in one calculation. For example, the problem:

$$3 + 10 - 2 \times 14 \div 7 = ?$$

has only one right answer! (Know what it is? It's 9.)

You can key the above problem directly, left to right, into your TI-30 type calculator with AOS entry method and you'll get the correct answer. *Not all calculators will do this.* A calculator with AOS (Algebraic Operating System) entry method, receives all the numbers and operations in the problem, automatically sorts them out for you, and applies them all according to the correct rules of mathematics – letting you see intermediate steps along the way. A calculator with AOS entry method automatically performs operations in the following order:

1) Single Variable Functions (the keys `sin` `cos` `tan` `log` `lnx` `x²` `√x` `1/x` `%` and `INV` working with them) act on the displayed number immediately. (All these keys are discussed for you later in this chapter). Then:
2) Exponentiation `yˣ`, and roots, $\sqrt[x]{y}$ (`INV` `yˣ`), are performed as soon as single variable functions are completed. (More on these functions later.)
3) Multiplications and divisions are completed next, then
4) Additions and subtractions are completed.

Finally, the equals key completes all operations.

In elementary school you may have heard the memory aid "My Dear Aunt Sally" (MDAS) applied to help you remember the last part of this hierarchy (multiplications and divisions first — in order left to right — then additions and subtractions in the same way). In a calculator equipped with AOS entry method — all of this is remembered for you. If your calculator does not have AOS entry method, you must apply the MDAS rule yourself.

There are cases in problem solving when *you* want to specify the order in which an expression is evaluated, or the way in which numbers and operations are grouped. In these cases you'd use the parentheses keys: ▢ ▢ , which are discussed in the next section. Parentheses always demand a special first level of attention in mathematics, and they are treated that way by your calculator. (Parentheses say "Do Me First".)

BASIC KEYS
( ) – The Parentheses Keys

In a variety of problems, you may need to specify the exact order in which expressions are evaluated, or the way in which numbers are grouped, as a problem is solved. The parentheses keys allow you to do this. Parentheses give you a way to "cluster" numbers and operations. By putting a series of numbers and operations in parentheses you tell the calculator: "Evaluate this little problem first – down to a single number result, then use this result for the rest of the calculation." You should make use of parentheses whenever you need the calculator to make an "intermediate" calculation, or if you have any doubts in your mind about how the calculator is going to reduce an expression.

Note that different calculators have different limits as to the number of parentheses that can be opened at any one time, and how many "pending" operations that can be handled. In a calculator of the TI-30 type, you can open up to 15 sets of parentheses at any one time, with up to 4 operations pending. Exceeding these limits results in an *Error* indication. (In this book, we will assume your calculation has two levels of parentheses.)

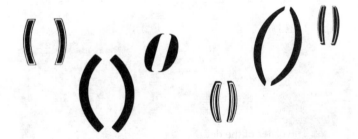

Notice the following important point when using parentheses. Often you'll see an equation or expression with parentheses indicating an *implied multiplication:* (2 + 1) (3 + 2) = 15. *Your calculator will not perform implied multiplications.* You have to key in the operation between parentheses:

⎡(⎤ 2 ⎡+⎤ 1 ⎡)⎤ ⎡×⎤ ⎡(⎤ 3 ⎡+⎤ 2 ⎡)⎤ ⎡=⎤ **15.**

Here's an example on the use of parentheses:

Evaluate: $\dfrac{(8 \times 4) + (9 \times -19)}{(3 + 10 \div 7) \times 2} =$

Solution: Here it's important that the calculator evaluates the entire numerator, and then divides by the entire denominator. In problems of this type, you can be sure of this by placing an extra set of parentheses around the numerator and denominator as you key in the problem.

Press

Press	Display/Comments
⎡(⎤ ⎡(⎤ 8 ⎡×⎤ 4 ⎡)⎤ ⎡+⎤	**32.** (8 × 4) displayed
⎡(⎤ 9 ⎡×⎤ 19 ⎡+/−⎤ ⎡)⎤ ⎡)⎤ ⎡÷⎤	**−139.** This is the value of the entire numerator
⎡(⎤ ⎡(⎤ 10 ⎡÷⎤ 7 ⎡+⎤ 3 ⎡)⎤	**4.4285714** This is (3 + 10 ÷ 7)
⎡×⎤ 2 ⎡)⎤	**8.8571429** This is the denominator.
⎡=⎤	**−15.693548** The final result. The ⎡=⎤ key completes the division and the entire problem.

Note: The order of the denominator was changed to follow the MDAS rule of algebraic hierarchy.

BASIC KEYS
EE↓ —
Scientific Notation

Very often, particularly in problems that relate to science or engineering, you find yourself needing to handle an astronomically huge or really small number. Such numbers are easily handled (by you and your calculator) using *scientific notation*. A number in scientific notation is expressed as a base number (or "mantissa") times ten raised to some power (or "exponent").

Mantissa × 10^power

(Raising a number to a power or exponent just means to multiply it by itself the number of times the power indicates: $10^3 = 10 \times 10 \times 10$.) To enter a number in scientific notation:

● Enter the mantissa (then press +/− if it's negative)
● Press EE↓ (EE stands for "Enter Exponent")
● Enter the power of ten (then press +/− if it's negative.)

A number such as −3.6089 × 10^32 will look like this in the calculator display:

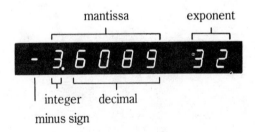

In scientific notation the power of *ten* tells you where the decimal point would have to be if you were going to write the number out longhand.

A positive exponent tells you how many places the decimal point should be shifted to the right.

Example: 2.9979×10^8 equals

299,790,000.

Move decimal 8 places right, add zeros as needed.

A negative exponent tells you how many places the decimal point should be shifted left.

Example: 1.6021×10^{-19} equals

.000 000 000 000 000 000 16021

Move decimal 19 places left, add zeros as needed.

It's easy to see why most folks prefer to handle very large and small numbers in Scientific Notation!

A few points on your calculator and scientific notation:

● No matter how you enter a mantissa the calculator will usually convert it to standard scientific form, with one digit to the left of the decimal point, when any function or operation key is pressed.

● Numbers in scientific notation can be mixed with numbers in standard form in any calculation.

Example: How many 0.5 meter footsteps are there from here to the moon? (Moon-Earth distance is approximately 3.8×10^8 meters)

Press

3.8 [EE↓] 8 [÷]
.5 [=]

Display/Comments

7.6   08
760 million footsteps!

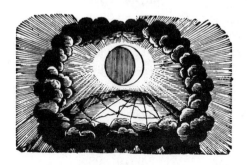

BASIC KEYS
[EE↓] and the
Exponential Shift

Some calculators have an [EE↓] key that allows you to shift the position of the decimal point when in scientific notation. Once you've entered a number in scientific notation, and pressed [=] or some other operation key, each push of the [EE↓] key *decreases* the exponent by 1, and moves the decimal point one place to the right. (This doesn't change the value of the number —just the way it looks.) In this way, you can explore how the position of the decimal point is related to the value of the exponent.

If you press [INV] [EE↓], just the reverse happens. The exponent goes up by one, and the decimal moves one place to the left. (The inverse key [INV], when present, works with several keys on your calculator, and will be discussed later on in this chapter.)

As an example, you might try exploring with the following numbers:

The speed of light is 2.9979250×10^8 m/sec.
How many million meters per second is that?

Press	Display/Comments
2.9979250 [EE↓] 8 [=]	**2.9979 08**
[EE↓]	**29.979 07**
[EE↓]	**299.79 06**
	Since one million is 1×10^6, the speed of light is over 299 million meters per second.
	Try moving things the other way with the [INV] [EE↓] sequence:
[INV] [EE↓]	**29.979 07**
[INV] [EE↓]	**2.9979 08**
[INV] [EE↓]	**.29979 09**
[INV] [EE↓]	**.02997 10**

With the [EE↓] and [INV] keys, you can put the decimal just about anywhere you'd want to in the mantissa. The exponent automatically changes to keep the value of the displayed number the same.

BASIC KEYS
$\boxed{1/x}$ — Inverse Function or "Reciprocal" Key

The $\boxed{1/x}$ key just takes the number in the display and divides it *into* 1. (By the way — the letter "x", used in calculator keys just means "any number that may be in the display.") The $\boxed{1/x}$ key can be used at any time: it acts immediately on whatever number is in the display, and doesn't affect other calculations in progress.

Now — why have a whole key just for $\boxed{1/x}$? Well, this operation is useful and important in a variety of problem solving situations:

Example:
You're trying to fill a swimming pool and want to speed up the process. You turn on a main fill faucet that would fill the pool by itself in 10 hours, set up a garden hose that would do it in 28 hours, and a fire hose that would take 6 hours on its own. How long does it take with all three working?

Solution:
$$\frac{1}{\text{Time Total}} = \frac{1}{T_1} + \frac{1}{T_2} + \frac{1}{T_3}$$
where T_1, T_2, and T_3 are the times for the faucet, garden hose and fire hose, respectively.

Press

10 $\boxed{1/x}$ $\boxed{+}$ 28 $\boxed{1/x}$ $\boxed{+}$
6 $\boxed{1/x}$ $\boxed{=}$ $\boxed{1/x}$

Display/Comments

3.3070866 hours, or about 3 hours, 18 minutes.

Note that the $\boxed{1/x}$ key "inverts" or flips over fractions; and this process can be useful in evaluating expressions you'll find in many situations — especially in basic science (see *Physics* section).

BASIC KEYS
STO RCL SUM EXC —
The Memory Keys

The memory in your calculator is a special place in the machine to store numbers you may need to use in calculations later on. It's sort of a "calculator within a calculator" since you can store numbers, or add to what's in memory, without affecting any other calculations you may have in progress. The CLEAR key will not clear out what's in memory.

STO — The "Store" key just "stores" the displayed number in the memory, without removing it from the display. (Any number previously stored in memory is *cleared out first.*)

By pressing
RCL — (Recall key) any time after a number is stored in memory, the number reappears on the display and can be used in operations and calculations. The number remains in the memory after you press the RCL key, and can be recalled as many times as you need it any time after that. The number will remain in memory until you alter it with one of the memory keys, or until you turn the calculator off. (Turning the calculator OFF and ON/C completely clears everything!)

Here's a quick example on the use of memory:

$$a = \frac{3}{8}(44 - 16)$$

$b = 144 - 9a,$ and you need to find b:

Press

3 ÷ 8 × (44 − 16)
= STO

144 − (9 × RCL) =

Display/Comments

10.5 The value for a, store it.

49.5 The value of b.

Another way of looking at memory is to consider that $\boxed{\text{RCL}}$ is a key that has a number value you can decide. If you need some weird number a lot of times in different calculations, just key it into your calculator and press $\boxed{\text{STO}}$. Every time you need it later on press $\boxed{\text{RCL}}$, and there it is!

$\boxed{\text{SUM}}$ or $\boxed{\text{M+}}$ — Key allows you to algebraically add whatever's in the display directly to what's in the memory. (On most calculators this doesn't affect any calculation in progress — check your owner's manual.) This key comes in handy when you want to keep a running total on something (say your grocery bill), while keeping the rest of the calculator clear for other things (such as calculating best unit prices or discounts).

$\boxed{\text{EXC}}$ — "Exchange" Key. This key "swaps" what's stored in memory with what's in the display. (The display value gets stored, while the stored number is recalled.) On most calculators this key doesn't affect any calculation in progress, and can come in handy in a variety of problem situations. Not all calculators have an Exchange key.

(If your calculator has multiple memories, your owner's manual will describe how to use them.)

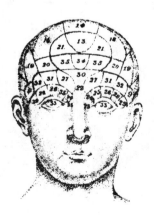

BASIC KEYS

 x^2 $\sqrt{x}$ — Square and Square Root Keys

The square key, x^2 , just takes the number in the display and multiplies it by itself.

This process, *squaring,* is a very handy one in a whole variety of situations in mathematics and in problems from everyday life — so your calculator has a whole key just for it.

One place squaring is handy is in calculating *areas.* For example, if you have a square field that is 5 kilometers on a side, its area is 5 squared (5^2) or 25 square kilometers.

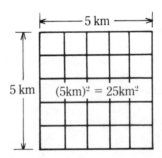

This illustration also suggests the origin of the term "square root" ($\sqrt{x}$). Let's say you have a *square* field that covers 25 square kilometers (25 km²) area and need to know how long it is on a side. Looking at the figure, you can see that the answer is 5 km. Well, the *square root* of 25 equals 5. You might say that the 5 km sides of the field give rise to its 25 km² area, in much the same way a "root" gives rise to a plant. Notice that the "$\sqrt{}$" symbol means square root, so you write the phrase "the square root of 25 is 5" simply: $\sqrt{25} = 5$.

The square root key $\boxed{\sqrt{x}}$ takes the square root of the number in the display. The square root of any number (say x) is another number ($\sqrt{x}$) that when multiplied by itself gives you back the original number. (Got that?)

Example: Evaluate:

$$\frac{(3 \times 8)}{\sqrt{2}} + 6 \times 3.1^2$$

Press   **Display/Comments**

3.1 $\boxed{x^2}$ $\boxed{\times}$ 6 $\boxed{=}$ $\boxed{+}$

$\boxed{(}$ $\boxed{(}$ 3 $\boxed{\times}$ 8 $\boxed{)}$ $\boxed{\div}$ 2 $\boxed{\sqrt{x}}$ $\boxed{)}$

$\boxed{=}$ **74.630563**

In expressions like those above, again notice that the $\boxed{x^2}$ and $\boxed{\sqrt{x}}$ functions do not act to complete a calculation that is not complete (such as 6×3.1) but *only* act on the number in the display. An "Error" indication will result if the $\boxed{\sqrt{x}}$ key is pressed with a negative number in the display. Square roots of negative numbers are called "imaginary" numbers, and your calculator is not equipped to handle these (see "Error" Indications section).

BASIC KEYS
$\boxed{y^x}$ and $\boxed{\text{INV}}$ $\boxed{y^x}$ —
Powers and Roots

A power (or "exponent") is a number that's written above and to the right of another number (called the base).

base — y^x — power or exponent

y^x just means:

Take the number y, and multiply it by itself x times — and that's just what the $\boxed{y^x}$ key does for you! This process is quite often required in problem solving, and can be a tedious process prone to all sorts of errors. With the $\boxed{y^x}$ key helping you, however, much of the hassle is eliminated.

To use the $\boxed{y^x}$ key just:
● Enter the base (y)
● Press $\boxed{y^x}$
● Enter the power (x)
● Press $\boxed{=}$

Example: You have a cubic bin that's exactly 3.21413 meters on a side. What's its volume in m³?

Solution:

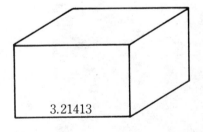

3.21413

The volume of the bin is 3.21413³.

Press

3.21413 $\boxed{y^x}$ 3 $\boxed{=}$

Display/Comments

33.203993 cubic meters

Important Note: On some calculators the right-most digit flashes during the short time the calculator is "grinding out" the result; on other calculators, the display goes blank. Be sure the calculator *has completely finished an operation* before pressing the next key!

Using the key sequence [INV] [y^x] gives you the "xth root of y", which is often written as $\sqrt[x]{y}$. The xth root of a number y, is another number ($\sqrt[x]{y}$), that when multiplied by itself x times, gives you back y. (Got that one?) Mathematically you would write:

$$(\sqrt[x]{y})^x = y.$$

This process of taking roots also crops up quite often in various applications of mathematics, and it's a downright "bear" of a task in many situations! With a calculator it's easy and accurate. To compute the xth root of y:

● Enter the base (y)
● Press [INV] [y^x]
● Enter the root (x)
● Press [=]

Example: Compute $\sqrt[3.12]{1460}$
(This would be tough, without your calculator)

Press   **Display/Comments**

1460 [INV] [y^x] 3.12 [=]   **10.332744**

If your calculator does not have an [INV] key, here is the procedure for taking the $\sqrt[x]{y}$:

Press   **Display/Comments**

1460 [y^x] 3.12 [$1/x$] [=]   **10.332744**

Additional important notes on [y^x] and [INV] [y^x] :
These two functions are the only special functions that do not act on the displayed value immediately. The second number (x value) must be entered in each case, before the function can be completed. The [=] key completes the calculation. (Closing a parenthesis that contains either of these functions will complete the operation also.)

On most calculators there is a restriction on these functions — the variable y should *not* be negative (this has to do with the way the calculator goes about computing the functions). If you try either of these with a negative number — you'll get an "Error" indication. (Trying to calculate a "zeroth" root also gives you an error!)

BASIC KEYS
$\boxed{K}$ — Calculations with a Constant

Here's a real labor-saving feature — one that can increase accuracy and reduce tedium when you've got to do a whole load of repetitive calculations. If your calculator has a $\boxed{K}$ constant key you can store *a number and an operation sequence,* and then these can be used by the calculator to operate on any displayed number. This type of feature is really handy if you have to "mark down" all the items in a store, or multiply all the ingredients in a recipe by 3, or in any repetitive situation!

To use the $\boxed{K}$ feature:
● Enter the repetitive number, m.
● Enter the desired operation.
● Press $\boxed{K}$.

From then on in, all you do is enter the string of numbers you want to operate on, and press $\boxed{=}$ after each entry to complete each calculation. The table below summarizes how the $\boxed{K}$ feature will work in each case:

m $\boxed{+}$ $\boxed{K}$	adds m to each subsequent entry, when $\boxed{=}$ is pressed.
m $\boxed{-}$ $\boxed{K}$	subtracts m from each subsequent entry.
m $\boxed{\times}$ $\boxed{K}$	multiplies each subsequent entry by m.
m $\boxed{\div}$ $\boxed{K}$	divides each subsequent entry by m.
m $\boxed{y^x}$ $\boxed{K}$	raises each subsequent entry to the m power.
m $\boxed{INV}$ $\boxed{y^x}$ $\boxed{K}$	takes the mth root of each subsequent entry.

Example: Multiply the numbers 81, 67, 21, 32 by .69174385.

Press	**Display/Comments**
.69174385 $\boxed{\times}$ $\boxed{K}$	Enter the repetitive number m and the operation ($\boxed{\times}$), then press $\boxed{K}$
81 $\boxed{=}$	**56.031252**
67 $\boxed{=}$	**46.346838**
21 $\boxed{=}$	**14.526621**
32 $\boxed{=}$	**22.135803**

Note: Clearing the calculator or entering any of the arithmetic functions clears the $\boxed{K}$ constant feature.
Some calculators have an automatic constant function that is activated by the $\boxed{=}$ key. Check your owner's manual
for details.

$\boxed{\pi}$ — "Pi" Key

The $\boxed{\pi}$ key, when pressed, displays the value of "π". (That's the Greek letter Pi, pronounced "pie".) The number you'll see in the display is 3.14159265... The quantity may actually be entered into your calculator correct to more digits, than shown in your display.

Pi is a very special number that represents a relationship that is found in *all circles*. The Greeks were the first to discover this relationship.

The Greeks probably studied thousands of circles before they determined the following fact: In any circle if you take the *distance around its edge* (called the circumference), and divide that by the *distance across its middle* (the diameter), the result is always the *same number*. That number is π, or about 3.1415927.

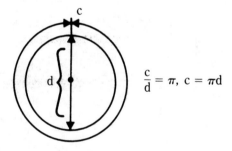

$$\frac{c}{d} = \pi, \ c = \pi d$$

π is found in almost any problem or calculation involving circles, and since circles are pretty common things a whole key on your calculator is devoted to remembering π for you. The $\boxed{\pi}$ key displays π immediately, does not affect calculations in progress, and can be used at any time in a calculation.

BASIC KEYS
% — Percent Key

Taxes, discounts, inflation, etc. all involve percentages —
the number of "cents per dollar" or parts per hundred. The
% key on your calculator is a genuine labor-saving device
that handles more than it appears to at first glance.

When the % key is pressed, the number in the display is
immediately converted to a decimal percent (multiplied by
0.01). If you enter 43.9 and press % , **0.439** appears
in the display.

The real power of an add-on % key is turned on when
it's used in combination with an operation key, which allows a
wide variety of percentage problems to be tackled. The
following key sequences, each operating on the displayed number, will handle the most common problems involving percentage.

+ n %   = adds n% to the number displayed.

Example: What will the cost of a new $75 jacket be with a
6.5% sales tax?

Press   **Display/Comments**

75 + 6.5 %   **4.875**   *Note:* At this point
                             6.5 per cent of 75 is computed
                             and displayed. Pressing =
                             adds this amount to 75 and
                             completes the calculation.

 =   **79.875**
                             (You'd pay $79.88).

Note: To work this problem without an *add-on* percent key
follow this procedure.

75 + (75 × .065)   = **79.875**

$\boxed{-}$ n $\boxed{\%}$ $\boxed{=}$ subtracts n% from the number displayed.

Example: You want to buy a stereo headset for $35; and a sale sign states 38% off. What's the actual price?

Press   **Display/Comments**

35 $\boxed{-}$ 38 $\boxed{\%}$ **13.3**   At this point, 38%
                                  of 35 is computed and
                                  displayed.
                                  Pressing $\boxed{=}$ subtracts it
                                  from 35 and completes the
                                  calculation.
$\boxed{=}$ **21.7**   (You'd get the phones
                                  for $21.70)

$\boxed{\times}$ n $\boxed{\%}$ $\boxed{=}$ multiplies the number in the display by n%.

This sequence is for straight percentage calculations:
What's 31.258% of $270.00?

Press   **Display/Comments**

270 $\boxed{\times}$ 31.258 $\boxed{\%}$ $\boxed{=}$ **84.3966**

$\boxed{\div}$ n $\boxed{\%}$ $\boxed{=}$ divides the displayed number by n%.

This key sequence helps to solve those "inverted" percentage problems.

Example: 25 is 15% of what number?

Press   **Display/Comments**

25 $\boxed{\div}$ 15 $\boxed{\%}$ $\boxed{=}$ **166.66667**

To figure percent without a $\boxed{\%}$ key, simply multiply the number by 0.01.

Press   **Display/Comments**

43.9 $\boxed{\times}$ .01 $\boxed{=}$ **0.439**

BASIC KEYS
DRG — Angular Measure Key

Angles are measurements that describe how 2 lines or surfaces meet each other. As discussed later on in the trigonometry section, angles are an important part of your life — and if you look around you you'll see angles everywhere.

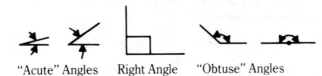

"Acute" Angles   Right Angle   "Obtuse" Angles

One common angle is the *right angle* (the angle at which walls meet floors), shown above. Angles smaller than right angles are called "acute", larger angles are called "obtuse."

There are 3 common sets of mathematical units you can use to specify angular measure, and they're all related to how they divide up a circle as follows:

The *degree:* $1° = 1/360$ of a circle

The *radian:* $1 \text{ rad} = \dfrac{1}{2\pi}$ of a circle

The *grad:* $1 \text{ grad} = \dfrac{1}{400}$ of a circle

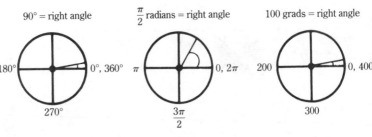

$90° = $ right angle $\dfrac{\pi}{2}$ radians = right angle 100 grads = right angle

$180°$ $0°, 360°$ π $0, 2\pi$ 200 $0, 400$

$270°$ $\dfrac{3\pi}{2}$ 300

$1° = \dfrac{1}{360}$ of a circle $1 \text{ radian} = \dfrac{1}{2\pi}$ of circle $1 \text{ grad} = \dfrac{1}{400}$ of circle

    Degrees   Radians   Grads

Many calculators can handle all three of these units and a DRG or similar key specifies which units the calculator assumes will be entered into its display. The DRG key works with the Trig functions (sin cos tan) described in the next section, and can be used with them to convert between systems of angular units.

The DRG key on a TI-30 type calculator is actually a 3-position switch that works as follows:

When your calculator is turned on, it is automatically in the degree mode.

Pressing DRG once puts the calculator in radian mode: an apostrophe (') at the left of the calculator display indicates this.

Pressing DRG once again puts the calculator in grad mode: a set of quotation marks (") at the left of the display indicates this mode.

(If you don't see an apostrophe or quotation marks at the left of the display — you're in degree mode.)

Be sure DRG is set correctly when solving Trig problems!

BASIC KEYS
sin cos tan — Trig Function Keys

Triangles! There are whole courses of study devoted to them.
Why? Well, triangles are very common shapes — found in a
variety of natural situations, they're ideal for certain construction
and architectural applications, part of inclined planes and
roadbeds, etc. In addition, the relationships between the sides
and angles of a right triangle (that's a triangle with one right
angle), crop up again and again in nature. The three
"trigonometric functions", called the *sine, cosine,* and *tangent,*
are an important part of the way scientists describe electrical
and wave phenomena, as well as many kinds of *periodic* motion
of mechanical systems.

The relationships are related to the right triangle as
shown below:

Hypotenuse

Opposite side

Θ

Adjacent side

The angle we'll focus on is Θ, and notice the side of the
triangle opposite to Θ is labelled *"Opposite"*, while the
side next to Θ is labelled *"Adjacent"*. The side opposite
to the right angle is called the *Hypotenuse.* The three
trigonometric functions are defined as follows:

$$\text{SIN } \Theta = \frac{\text{Length of Opposite Side}}{\text{Length of Hypotenuse}} = \frac{O}{H}$$

$$\text{COS } \Theta = \frac{\text{Length of Adjacent Side}}{\text{Length of Hypotenuse}} = \frac{A}{H}$$

$$\text{TAN } \Theta = \frac{\text{Length of Opposite Side}}{\text{Length of Adjacent Side}} = \frac{O}{A}$$

The sin cos and tan keys each assume that there is an
angle in the display, *in units specified by the setting of
the* DRG *key.* When any of these 3 keys are pressed, the ap-
propriate function (sine, cosine, or tangent) of the displayed angle is computed and displayed immediately. These
3 keys do not affect calculations in progress, and can be
used at any time.

Example: Compute the sine, cosine, and tangent of 90 degrees and 90 grads.

Press   **Display/Comments**

[OFF] [ON/C]   This makes certain the cal-
                          culator is in degree mode.
90 [sin]   **1.**
90 [cos]   **0.**
90 [tan]   **Error.**   (The tangent of
                          90° is undefined.)
[ON/C]   Clears "Error" condition.
[DRG] [DRG]   *"* **0.**   Converts to grads
                                       mode.
90 [sin]   *"***.98768834**
90 [cos]   *"***.15643447**
90 [tan]   *"***6.3137515**

The "ARC" trigonometric functions – ARCSINE,
ARCCOSINE and ARCTANGENT,
are the trigonometric functions in "reverse." The term *Arc-sine* (often written sin⁻¹) means "The Angle whose SINE is."
You calculate arcsines, arccosines, and arctangents using the
[INV] key, with the [sin] [cos] and [tan] keys on your calculator. The result of an "arc" calculation is an angle, that
will be in the units specified by the setting of the [DRG] key.

[INV] [sin] – Calculates the smallest angle whose sine is in the
display (first or fourth quadrant).

[INV] [cos] – Calculates the smallest angle whose cosine is
in the display (first or second quadrant).

[INV] [tan] – Calculates the smallest angle whose tangent is
in the display (first or fourth quadrant). (For more information on these key sequences – see Chapter 6.)

Examples: Calculate the arcsin of 0.514
                       arccos of 1.4
            and arctan of 15, all in degrees.

Press   **Display/Comments**

[OFF] [ON/C]   This makes sure you're in degree
                          mode.
.514 [INV] [sin]   **30.930637** degrees
1.4 [INV] [cos]   **Error.**   *Note:* The argument of
                          the sine or cosine is always be-
                          tween plus and minus 1.
15 [INV] [tan]   **86.185925** degrees.

BASIC KEYS

log lnx —
Logarithm Keys

Logarithms, or "Logs" as they are commonly called, were originally worked up by mathematicians to make computations easier (much as calculators have been devised today). Logarithmic functions have gone on to be involved in man's mathematical descriptions of many natural phenomena. They are found to be helpful describing many natural effects — so you'll be seeing them in a variety of situations.

Logarithms are related to exponential functions, and work like this: If you pick a number called a base (b) then any other number, (say x) can be expressed as b raised to some power (y).

$$x = b^y$$

The logarithm is the *inverse* of this exponential function, and may be written:

$$y = \log_b x.$$

which is stated: "y equals log to the base b of x."

Now why all of this? Logs are very useful (your calculator even uses them internally) in handling complex problems, because using logs allows multiplication, division, and exponentiation (raising to a power) to be replaced by the simpler operations of addition, subtraction and multiplication. The rules for math with logs are as follows;

$\log_b(xy) = \log_b(x) + \log_b(y)$

$\log_b (x/y) = \log_b x - \log_b (y)$

$\log_b (x^n) = n \log_b x$

To do math with logs (before your calculator came along) you would first look up logarithms of the numbers x and y (in bulky tables), perform the operations you need, longhand, according to the rules above, then take the *antilogarithm* (using tables again) of your results to get your final answers.

There are two common bases used for logarithms, and hence your calculator's two log keys. Logarithms to the base 10 are convenient for use in calculating, and are called the *common* logarithms. The log key on your calculator immediately displays the common logarithm (base 10) of the number in the display.

The other common base for logarithms is a special number called "e", whose value is 2.7182818 .... Logs with this base are called the *natural* logarithms, and occur in many formulas in higher mathematics. (Natural logs are often abbreviated "ln x".)The [lnx] key on your calculator immediately displays the natural logarithm (base e) of the number in the display.

Note: When calculating logarithms with either the [log] or [lnx] keys, the number in the display must be *positive*, or an "Error" indication will result.

The [INV] key works with the [log] and [lnx] keys to calculate *antilogarithms:*

The common antilogarithm (10 to the x power) sequence [INV] [log] calculates the common antilogarithm of the displayed value. This sequence raises 10 to the displayed power.

The natural antilogarithm (e to the x power) sequence [INV] [lnx] calculates the natural antilogarithm of the number in the display. This sequence raises the number e to the displayed power.

Examples:
Calculate: log 15.32
$\qquad$ ln 203.451
$\qquad$ $e^{-.693}$
$\qquad$ 10^{π}

Press
15.32 [log]
203.451 [lnx]
.693 [+/−] [INV] [lnx]
[π] [INV] [log]

Display/Comments
1.1852588
5.3154252
0.5000736
1385.4557

BASIC KEYS
INV — Inverse Key Summary

The inverse key has been mentioned throughout this chapter in each situation where it can work in a sequence with other keys. Here is a summary of where it works and what it does.

[INV] [EE↓] adds one to the exponent and moves the decimal one place to the left.

[INV] [y^x] takes the xth root of the displayed value y. Order of entry is y [INV] [y^x] x. y cannot be negative, but both x and y can be fractional.

[INV] [sin] Arcsine ($\sin^{-1}$) Sequence — Calculates the smallest angle whose sine is in the display (first or fourth quadrant).

[INV] [cos] Arccosine ($\cos^{-1}$) Sequence — Calculates the smallest angle whose cosine is in the display (first or second quadrant).

[INV] [tan] Arctangent ($\tan^{-1}$) Sequence — Calculates the smallest angle whose tangent is in the display (first or fourth quadrant).

[INV] [log] Common Antilogarithm (10 to the x power) Sequence — Calculates the common antilogarithm of the displayed value (raises 10 to the displayed power).

[INV] [lnx] Natural Antilogarithm (e to the x power) Sequence — Calculates the natural antilogarithm of the number in the display (raises e to the displayed power).

BASIC KEYS
"Error" Indications

If your calculator displays an "Error" indication, you probably asked it to try to do something it couldn't do. (It tries to do everything you ask it to; when it can't, it signals for help with the "Error" Signal.)

When this occurs, no entry from the keyboard is accepted until your calculator is cleared or turned off and on again. This clears the error condition and all pending operations. Then, you have to begin the problem from scratch — starting right at the top. Here are typical reasons why you'll get an "Error" message:

1. Number entry or calculation result (including summa-tion into memory) outside the range of the calculator.
2. Dividing a number by zero.
3. The mantissa is zero and $\boxed{\text{log}}$, $\boxed{\text{ln}x}$ or $\boxed{1/x}$ is pressed.
4. The mantissa is negative and $\boxed{\text{log}}$, $\boxed{\sqrt{x}}$, $\boxed{y^x}$, $\boxed{\text{ln}x}$ or $\boxed{\text{INV}}$ $\boxed{y^x}$ is pressed.
5. Inverse of sine or cosine (arcsine, arccosine) when the mantissa is greater than 1.
6. Tangent of 90°, 270°, $\pi/2$, $3\pi/2$, 100 grads, 300 grads or their rotation multiples like 450°, etc.

   Check your owner's manual for "Error" messages unique to your calculator.

1-33

KEYING UP CONVERSIONS
Introduction

Everything that's measured or measurable needs some sort of
unit to be measured in. Folks need to know how far, how long,
how fast, and how much — in terms they'll recognize and
agree on. Up until quite recently folks in the U.S. were
using the "English" system of units, where distances were
measured in feet (or miles), forces were measured in pounds,
and gasoline was bought by the gallon. Now the *metric* system
is being adopted, in which lengths are in meters, mass is in
kilograms, and gas is bought by the liter. For awhile, having
to convert between these two systems of units will be a common
situation.

Changing units from the English system to the metric system
will be very easy with this book and your calculator. All you
do is press the correct keys.

KEYING UP CONVERSIONS
Use of
Alphabetical Table

An alphabetical table of units is contained in Appendix 1.
This table contains many uncommon as well as common units.
Most units in this list are related to several other units
(both metric and English).

An example: Find the number of square meters in 0.5 acres.
Procedure: You know the number of acres so look up acres in
the alphabetical table. Note that this table shows how to
convert acres to square feet, square yards, and square miles,
as well as square meters. From the table, acres ☒ 4047 ⊜
square meters.

Press

0.5 ☒ 4047 ⊜

Display/Comments

2023.5
There are 2023.5 square
meters in 0.5 acres.

You may want to make up a few problems of your own and use this
table until you feel comfortable with it.

Common Conversions

The following two tables will allow conversions of commonly used units. The first table gives conversions from English to metric units. For example, the first listing states: inches ⊠ 2.540 ⊟ centimeters. This would allow you to quickly handle a conversion such as: "How many centimeters are contained in 8 inches?"

Press

8 ⊠ 2.540 ⊟

Display/Comments

20.32   That's all there is to it! There are 20.32 centimeters in 8 inches.

Another example: "How many yards long is a 100 meter football field?" Look at the metric to English conversion table since the number of meters is given. Also, note that the meter is a unit of length, so look in the length section. You should find meters ⊠ 1.0936 ⊟ yards.

Press

100 ⊠ 1.0936 ⊟

Display/Comments

109.36   In other words, a 100-meter football field will be 109.36 yards in length.

The metric unit for temperature is degrees Celsius. Although conversions involving temperature are not as simple as length conversions, they can be done easily with your calculator.

Note that (°F) means degrees Fahrenheit and (°C) means degrees Celsius. If body temperature is 98.6°F, how many °C is it? Look at the table under temperature conversions (English to metric). You should see Fahrenheit (°F) ⊟ 32 ⊟ ⊠ 5 ÷ 9 ⊟ Celsius (°C).

Press

98.6 ⊟ 32 ⊟ ⊠ 5 ÷ 9 ⊟

Display/Comments

37.   Body temperature is 37° Celsius.

KEYING UP CONVERSIONS
English to Metric Table

Length

inches	✕ 2.540	= centimeters
feet	✕ 30.48	= centimeters
yards	✕ 91.44	= centimeters
yards	✕ 0.9144	= meters
miles	✕ 1.609	= kilometers

Area

square inches	✕ 6.452	= square centimeters
square inches	✕ 645.2	= square millimeters
square feet	✕ 929.0	= square centimeters
square yards	✕ 0.8361	= square meters
acres	✕ 4047	= square meters
square miles	✕ 2.590	= square kilometers

Volume (U.S.)

pints	✕ 0.4732	= liters
quarts	✕ 0.9464	= liters
gallons	✕ 3785	= cubic centimeters
gallons	✕ 3.785	= liters
cubic inches	✕ 16.39	= cubic centimeters

Weight

pounds	✕ 4.448	= newtons
pounds	✕ 0.4536	= kilogram force
tons (short)	✕ 907.2	= kilogram force
tons (short)	✕ 0.9072	= tons (metric)

Power

horsepower	✕ 0.7457	= kilowatts

Energy

British thermal units	✕ 1055	= joules
British thermal units	✕ 2.930×10^{-4}	= kilowatt-hours

Angle Measures

degrees	✕ 0.01745	= radians
degrees	✕ 1.111	= grads

Temperature

Fahrenheit (°F)	− 32 =	
	✕ 5 ÷ 9	= Celsius (°C)

KEYING UP CONVERSIONS
Metric to English Table

Length

centimeters	✖ 0.3937	= inches
centimeters	✖ 0.0328	= feet
centimeters	✖ 0.0109	= yards
meters	✖ 1.0936	= yards
kilometers	✖ 0.6215	= miles

Area

square centimeters	✖ 0.1550	= square inches
square millimeters	✖ 0.00153	= square inches
square centimeters	✖ 0.001076	= square feet
square meters	✖ 1.1960	= square yards
square meters	✖ 2.471×10^{-4}	= acres
square kilometers	✖ 0.3861	= square miles

Volume (U.S.)

liters	✖ 2.1133	= pints
liters	✖ 1.0567	= quarts
cubic centimeters	✖ 2.642×10^{-4}	= gallons
liters	✖ 0.2642	= gallons
cubic centimeters	✖ 0.0610	= cubic inches

Weight

newtons	✖ 0.2248	= pounds
kilogram force	✖ 2.2046	= pounds
kilogram force	✖ 0.00110	= tons (short)
tons (metric)	✖ 1.1023	= tons (short)

Power

kilowatts	✖ 1.3410	= horsepower

Energy

joules	✖ 9.478×10^{-4}	= British thermal units
kilowatt hours	✖ 3413.1	= British thermal units

Angle measures

radians	✖ 57.30	= degrees
grads	✖ 0.900	= degrees

Temperature

Celsius (°C)	✖ 9 ÷ 5 + 32	= Fahrenheit (°F)

2-5

KEYING UP CONVERSIONS
Making
a Factor

This method of making conversions is helpful when complex units are being handled, since it allows many steps to be systematically recorded. This method is based on what happens to a quantity multiplied by one. Does the quantity change in value? No, but it may be converted to another system of units. For instance, to change 1 foot to inches you would multiply by 12. This can be thought of as 1 foot $\times \left(\dfrac{12 \text{ inches}}{1 \text{ foot}} \right) = 12$ inches.

Thus $\left(\dfrac{12 \text{ inches}}{1 \text{ foot}} \right)$ is a conversion factor for feet to inches.

A conversion factor is a quantity which is equal to one and relates two units.

Most people agree that $\left(\dfrac{1 \text{ meter}}{1 \text{ meter}} \right)$ is equal to one. Also it is true that 1 meter represents 3.281 feet, so whenever you see 1 meter you may replace it by an equivalent 3.281 feet. For instance, the quantity $\left(\dfrac{1 \text{ meter}}{1 \text{ meter}} \right)$ is the same as $\left(\dfrac{1 \text{ meter}}{3.281 \text{ feet}} \right)$ which is the same as $\left(\dfrac{3.281 \text{ feet}}{1 \text{ meter}} \right)$. The quantity $\left(\dfrac{1 \text{ meter}}{3.281 \text{ feet}} \right)$ can be used to change feet to meters, and $\left(\dfrac{3.281 \text{ feet}}{1 \text{ meter}} \right)$ can be used to change meters to feet. For instance, "How many meters are contained in 50 feet?"

The conversion factor needs to "cancel" feet so the form to be used is

$50 \text{ feet} \times \left(\dfrac{1 \text{ meter}}{3.281 \text{ feet}} \right) =$ You may complete this conversion with your calculator.

Press

50 ☒ 3.281 🗌 ☐

Display/Comments

15.239256   There are about 15.2 meters in 50 feet.

KEYING UP CONVERSIONS
Data for Making a Factor

When you're making conversions using conversion factors you need only a few basic facts. The following list will enable you to perform many conversions including those you'll find necessary in the study of chemistry and physics. Using these facts, and your calculator, could save you the trouble of hunting through a long list of conversions.

Distance, Area, and Volume Conversions

1 m = 3.2808399 ft
1 m = 1.0936133 yd
1 km = 0.62137119 mi
1 cm = 0.39370079 in.

Mass and Weight Conversions

1 kg = 2.2046226 lb
  (approximate on earth)
1 g = 0.03527396 oz
  (approximate on earth)
1 N = 0.224 lb
1 kg = 0.0685 slugs
1 metric ton = 1.1023113
  short tons

Power and Efficiency Conversions

1 kw = 1.341003 hp
1 kw hr = 2.656×10^6 ft-lb
1 Joule = 9.480×10^{-4} Btu
1 erg = 7.3756103×10^{-8} ft-lb
1 m/s = 2.2369363 mi/h

1 km/h = 0.62137119 mi/h
1 km/l = 2.3521458 mi/gal
1 cal-gram = 3.96832×10^{-3} Btu
1 Pascal (N-m²) = 1.45136×10^{-4} lb/in.²
$^\circ C = \frac{5}{9} (^\circ F - 32)$ and $^\circ F = \frac{9}{5} \, ^\circ C + 32$

Miscellaneous Conversions

1 mi = 5280 ft
1 mi = 0.86897624 naut. mi
1 mi/h = 0.86897624 knots
1 hp-h = 1.98×10^6 ft-lb
1 joule = 2.777×10^{-7} kw-h
1 in. of Hg = 3.342×10^{-2} atm
1 lb/in.² = 6.804×10^{-2} atm
1 ft-lb = 1.285×10^{-3} Btu
1 gal = 231.0 cu.in.
1 hp = 550 ft-lb/s
1 fl.oz = 0.125 cups
1 cup = 16 tbs
1 tbs = 3 tsp
1 lb = 16 oz
1 gal = 4 qt
1 qt = 2 pints
1 pint = 2 cups
1 cord = 128 ft³
1 radian = 57.2958°
1° = 1.1111 grads
1m² = 10^4 cm²
1 Angstrom = 10^{-10}m

KEYING UP CONVERSIONS
Metric Factors and Examples

Now for a more complex example: Let's say you have to convert 0.2 meters per second to miles per hour. Use the information 1 meter = 3.281 feet, 5280 feet = 1 mile, 60 seconds = 1 minute, and 60 minutes = 1 hour.

Start by writing the data in the units you're given, and then multiply by the necessary conversion factors until you get the units you want.

$$0.2 \, \frac{\text{meters}}{\text{second}} \times \frac{3.281 \text{ feet}}{1 \text{ meter}} \times \frac{1 \text{ mile}}{5280 \text{ feet}} \times \frac{60 \text{ seconds}}{1 \text{ minute}} \times \frac{60 \text{ minutes}}{1 \text{ hour}}$$

The remaining units are $\frac{\text{mile(s)}}{\text{hour}}$ as desired. You may complete this conversion with your calculator.

Press

0.2 ☒ 3.281 ☒ 5280 ☑
☒ 60 ☒ 60 ▱

Display/Comments

0.44740909 so 0.2 meters/second is about 0.45 miles/hour

If you will be converting $\frac{\text{meters}}{\text{second}}$ to $\frac{\text{miles}}{\text{hour}}$ quite often you might want to design a conversion factor. All that is necessary is to multiply the conversion factors without the given data.

Press

3.281 ☒ 5280 ☑
☒ 60 ☒ 60 ▱

Display/Comments

2.2370455   Probably you will need accuracy to only 2.23"

so $\frac{\text{meters}}{\text{second}}$ ☒ 2.237 ▱ $\frac{\text{miles}}{\text{hour}}$.

Conversions within the Metric System

Conversions within the metric system are easily handled since the names of the units carry descriptive prefixes. For example, kilo means 1000 so a *kilo*meter is *1000* meters or 1 kilometer = 1000 meters. The resulting conversion factors are

$\left(\dfrac{1 \text{ kilometer}}{1000 \text{ meters}}\right)$ and $\left(\dfrac{1000 \text{ meters}}{1 \text{ kilometer}}\right)$. Looking at another example, *Centi* means 0.01, so a *centi*meter is *0.01* meter.
The resulting conversion factors are $\left(\dfrac{1 \text{ centimeter}}{0.01 \text{ meter}}\right)$
and $\left(\dfrac{0.01 \text{ meter}}{1 \text{ centimeter}}\right)$.

Metric System Prefixes

Prefix	Numerical Meaning	Example	Symbol
Tera	10^{12}	Terameter	Tm
Mega	10^{6}	Megaliters	Ml
kilo	10^{3}	kilograms	kg
hecto	10^{2}	hectoliter	hl
deka	10	dekagram	dag
		meter	m
deci	10^{-1}	deciliter	dl
centi	10^{-2}	centimeter	cm
milli	10^{-3}	milliliter	ml
micro	10^{-6}	microgram	μg
nano	10^{-9}	nanometer	nm
pico	10^{-12}	picometer	pm

Example: How many cubic millimeters are there in 2 cubic meters?
A *milli*meter is 10^{-3} meters, or 1 millimeter $= 10^{-3}$ meters.
so the conversion factor to change meters to millimeters is
$\left(\dfrac{1 \text{ millimeter}}{10^{-3} \text{ meters}}\right)$. Now to convert cubic meters the conversion factor

must be cubed. Remember $\left(\dfrac{a}{bc}\right)^{3} = \left(\dfrac{a}{bc}\right)\left(\dfrac{a}{bc}\right)\left(\dfrac{a}{bc}\right) = \dfrac{a^{3}}{b^{3}c^{3}}$.

The conversion factor cubed is $\left(\dfrac{1 \text{ millimeter}}{10^{-3} \text{ meters}}\right)^{3} = \dfrac{1 \text{ millimeter}^{3}}{(10^{-3})^{3} \text{ meters}^{3}}$
Multiply the 2 cubic meters in the problem by the conversion
factor. (Remember $10^{-3} = 1 \times 10^{-3}$.)

$$2 \text{ meters}^{3} \times \dfrac{1 \text{ millimeter}^{3}}{(10^{-3})^{3} \text{ meters}^{3}} =$$

Press

2 ⊡ ⦅ 1 [EE↨] 3 [+/−] [y˟]

3 ⦆ ⊟

Display/Comments

2. 09 There are
2 billion mm^{3} in 2m^{3}.

KEYS TO HOME MANAGEMENT
Introduction

Your calculator can be a powerful tool to keep handy for
many everyday activities. Calculating best buys, checking on sales tax, keeping the checkbook balanced, or
planning home projects are all made easier and more accurate with your calculator. We've tried to include examples in
this chapter that cover a wide spectrum of "round the house"
situations, as well as those calculations you come up against in
stores, auto service stations, banks, hardware and building
supply houses, etc. Why leave it to the salesclerk (or to chance)
when you can check and be sure?

KEYS TO HOME MANAGEMENT
Balancing
Your Checkbook

Each month when the bank sends you a statement of your account,
sit down and take a few minutes to balance your checkbook.
What you're really doing is just making sure that you and
your bank agree about just how much of your money they have.
With your calculator, you'll get a fast and accurate picture.

When the bank's statement arrives, it will have a list of deposits, withdrawals, and miscellaneous charges or credits.
Check these against your record. When you have done this,
there will probably be some checks which have not yet been
paid by the bank (checks outstanding); some deposits may not
yet be accounted for (deposits in transit), and there may be
some service charges that you have not yet deducted from your
checkbook balance (bank debit memos). To balance your check-
book: (Statement Balance $\boxed{+}$ Deposits in Transit $\boxed{-}$ Checks Outstanding) $\boxed{=}$ (Checkbook Balance $\boxed{-}$ Debit Memos).

Use this information to reconcile this account:
Balance in checkbook record = \$209.15
Balance shown on statement = \$940.96
Checks outstanding = #119 (76.83), #131 (122.87), #132
(219.50), #133 (397.31), #134 (231.00), #135 (138.25).
Debit memo = \$3.95   Deposits in transit = \$450.00

Press	Display/Comments
209.15 $\boxed{-}$ 3.95 $\boxed{=}$	**205.2** First, enter any debit memos into your checkbook record and subtract from your balance to get your *New Checkbook Balance:* \$205.20. (The tally on the rest of your account should agree with this.)

Add your statement balance to your deposits in transit and store:

940.96 ⊞ 450.00 ⊟ STO

1390.96

Next, add up all your checks outstanding:

76.83 ⊞ 122.87 ⊞ 219.50 ⊞
397.31 ⊞ 231.00 ⊞ 138.25 ⊟

1185.76

Subtract this from memory (make it negative and press SUM).

+/− SUM

RCL

205.2   This agrees with your new checkbook balance — your account is O.K.

Try it on your own checkbook. Common errors might be made re-cording a check or deposit amount incorrectly, totalling wrong, or forgetting to record a check or deposit.

Here's a trick to help find mistakes — if your checkbook bal-ance and statement balance differ by an amount that is even-ly divisible by 9, chances are that your error is one of transposing two numbers (i.e., recording 54 instead of 45, or 329 instead of 239).

Payday

The type of work you do usually determines how your salary is calculated. Check on it with your calculator!

Example:
Find your gross weekly wages for the following situations.

a) You work at a bakery for $2.75 an hour. You work 4-1/2 hours per day Monday through Friday. Saturday you work 8 hours regular plus 3 hours overtime at 1-1/2 times the straight time rate.

Total pay = (Hourly pay × hours worked) + (overtime hours × overtime rate × hourly pay)

Press	**Display/Comments**
2.75 ⊠ ⊏	Hourly pay
4.5 ⊠ 5 ⊞ 8 ⊐	**30.5** hours regular time
⊜ STO	**83.875** Regular time pay
3 ⊠ 1.5 ⊠ 2.75	
⊞ RCL ⊜	**96.25** Total pay for the week.

b) You work on a potato farm. You are paid 55¢ per box of potatoes. You pick boxes of potatoes for the week as follows:

Monday:	54	Thursday:	49
Tuesday:	63	Friday:	58
Wednesday:	56	Saturday:	52

Equation: Total boxes × amount per box = wages

Press	**Display/Comments**
54 ⊞ 63 ⊞ 56 ⊞	
49 ⊞ 58 ⊞ 52 ⊜	**332.** boxes
⊠ .55 ⊜	**182.6** (wages)

c) You work on a base salary of $800.00 per month plus commission of 4.25% on all sales over $900.00. Your sales for the month are $1,328.57.

Equation: Base salary + (sales − 900) × commission rate = Total pay.

Press	**Display/Comments**
800 ⊞	Base salary
⊏ ⊏ 1328.57 ⊟ 900 ⊐	**428.57** (Sales over $900
⊠ ⊏ 4.25 ⊠ .01 ⊐ ⊐ ⊜	**818.21** Total pay

Keys to Good Cooking — Recipe Conversions

Often you may have a recipe for something good, but find that you need more or less of the final product than it specifies. Your calculator makes recipe conversions quick, accurate and easy.

For example:
In a recipe, you need (among other things) 2-1/3 cups of flour, 1-1/4 cups of sugar, 4 tablespoons of chocolate, and 3/4 cup of water. You want to make 1/3 of this recipe.

> Original recipe ingredient quantity $\div$ 3 $=$
> New (1/3) ingredient quantity

(Remember that dividing by 3 is the same as multiplying by 1/3).

Press	**Display/Comments**
1 $\div$ 3 $=$ STO	**.33333333** First, store 1/3 in memory.
2 $+$ 3 1/x $=$	**2.3333333** Enter the amount of flour, and multiply by RCL to get new amount:
$\times$ RCL $=$	**.77777778** cups of *flour*
1 $+$ .4 1/x $=$	**1.25**
$\times$ RCL $=$	**.41666667** cups of *sugar*
4 $\times$ RCL $=$	**1.3333333** tbs. of *chocolate*
3 $\div$ 4 $\times$ RCL $=$	**.25** cups of *water*

So, you would need 3/4 cup (plus a little more) flour, about halfway between 1/3 and 1/2 cup of sugar, 1-1/3 tablespoons (1 tbs + 1 tsp) of chocolate, and 1/4 cup of water.

KEYS TO HOME MANAGEMENT
Diet Planning
— On Keys

Diets often involve careful planning, which your calculator can make easier and more accurate (especially if metric units are involved.) *Here's an example:*

Your ideal weight is 60.7 kg (about 134 lb). You weigh 70 kg (about 154 lb). Since you're an active person, you require about 44 calories of food energy per day for every kilogram of body weight. To lose 1 kilogram per week of body weight you must cut your weekly calorie intake by 9,720 calories. To get to your ideal weight in 12 weeks, how many calories must you have per day?

Here are the formulas you'll need:
Weight ⌐−⌐ ideal weight ⌐=⌐ required loss
Loss (kg) ⌐÷⌐ weeks ⌐=⌐ kg loss per week
Kg loss per week ⌐×⌐ weekly calories to cut ⌐=⌐ Calories to cut each
     to lose 1 kg   week to lose weight

Calories to cut per week ⌐÷⌐ days in week ⌐=⌐ Calories to
     cut per day

44 Calories ⌐×⌐ Ideal weight ⌐=⌐ Weight maintenance level
     (calories)

Weight maintenance level ⌐−⌐ Calories to cut ⌐=⌐ Total
     (calories)   to lose weight   calories
                                              per day

Press	Display/Comments
70 ⌐−⌐ 60.7 ⌐=⌐	**9.3** kg (Required loss)
⌐÷⌐ 12 ⌐=⌐	**0.775** kg (Required loss per week for 12 weeks)
⌐×⌐ 9,720 ⌐=⌐	**7533.** fewer calories per week
⌐÷⌐ 7 ⌐=⌐ STO	**1076.1429** fewer calories per day
44 ⌐×⌐ 60.7 ⌐=⌐	**2670.8** calories/day (maintenance level)
⌐−⌐ RCL ⌐=⌐	**1594.6571** (1595 calories/day)

3-6

To plan a balanced menu, use a chart. Allow one gm of protein for each kg of ideal body weight (so, you require 61 grams of protein). You must carefully calculate foods and portion sizes to limit calorie intake. Here's a sample.

Breakfast	Calories	Protein (g)
(150 g medium orange)	68	1.4
1 thin slice crisp toast (23 g)	65	1.6
1 boiled egg (54 g)	77	6.1
skim milk (246 g)	87	8.6
	297	17.7

Lunch		
240 g clear soup (broth)	9	2.0
113 g small serving fillet of sole	135	16.9
1 slice bread	65	1.6
Large serving green salad w/lemon juice	15	.6
120 grams cottage cheese	108	22.0
1 medium apple (25g)	72	.4
	404	43.5

Dinner		
Bowl clear soup	50	2.0
Medium hamburger (80 g)	291	17.6
1 serving green beans (100 g)	22	1.4
1 small potato (boiled) (100 g)	83	2.0
Tossed salad w/low calorie dressing	50	1.2
120 g gelatin	86	1.7
Glass whole milk (244 g)	166	8.5
	748	34.4

Total

Protein = 95.6
Calories = 1449

KEYS TO HOME MANAGEMENT
Credit Card
Buying

When making a large purchase, especially one that may involve some credit buying, it may be very worthwhile to spend a few minutes with your calculator first. Play "what if" on keys! Try some alternatives. Be satisfied that the whole purchase, including any costs of credit, is a good deal before committing your money. *Here's an example:*

You are buying a 4-piece stereo component system at a large department store. The cost is $559.95. You decide to charge the purchase on the store's revolving charge account. The following rates and minimum payments apply:

Unpaid Balance	Monthly Interest Rate	Balance	Minimum Payment
0 - $500	1-1/2%	Under $200	$10
Over $500	1%	Over $200	5% of new balance

To find the opening balance, interest and minimum payment for a six-month period:

Balance × Monthly Interest Rate = Monthly Interest
Balance + Monthly Interest = Unpaid Balance
Unpaid Balance × 5% = Minimum monthly Payment (for amounts over $200)
Unpaid Balance − Minimum Monthly Payment = Balance (for next month)

Press	Display/Comments
559.95 ➕ 1 〔 559.95	
✕ .01 〕	**5.5995** (At this point the display reads out 1% of 559.95 − your first month's interest, $5.60).
🟰	**565.5495** (Unpaid Balance = $565.55)
✕ .05 🟰 STO	**28.277475** (Minimum Payment = $28.28)
565.55 ➖ RCL 🟰	**537.27253** Balance (for 2nd month) = $537.27

Repeat this sequence for six months and put in chart form as shown here:

Month	Opening Balance	Interest	Unpaid Balance	Minimum Payment
1	559.95	5.60 (1%)	565.55	28.28
2	537.27	5.37 (1%)	542.64	27.13
3	515.51	5.16 (1%)	520.67	26.03
4	494.64	7.42 (1-1/2%)	502.06	25.10
5	476.96	7.15 (1-1/2%)	484.11	24.21
6	459.90	6.90 (1-1/2%)	466.80	23.34

Notice the difference in interest in the fourth month. Also, notice the amount of interest you will have already paid — after only six months, it already totals $37.60! And you've only paid for about $100 of the cost of the stereo! Try contrasting the cost of this credit card purchase of the stereo with the cost of taking out a short term loan to purchase it.

Sometimes, sale "bargains" are not bargains at all. If a stereo you want is on sale for $525, marked down from $600, you may pay less by waiting to save the $600 than paying the sale price plus interest.

Grocery Shopping on Limited Budget

Have you ever gone to the grocery store with your very last ten dollar bill? You carefully pick and choose your products until you get close to $10, hoping that the adding on of tax will not exceed your limit. With your calculator, you can calculate exactly what the bill will be.

You have in your basket items priced at $0.17, 3.22, 4.10, 1.06, .89, and .45; and a 6.5% tax to pay. Did you get too much? If you wanted to take back just one item to make the total less than $10 (but as large as possible), which item should you take back? How much change would you get from a $10 bill?

Press	Display/Comments
.17 + 3.22 + 4.1	
+ 1.06 + .89	
+ .45 =	**9.89** Subtotal
+ (9.89 × .065)	**0.64285** (tax)
=	**10.53285** Total = $10.53 (too much)
9.89 − .89 =	**9.** (Take back .89 item Subtotal = $9.00)
+ (9 × .065) =	**9.585** Total: $9.59
+/− + 10	
=	**0.415** Your change. Notice the 9.585 becomes 9.59 and the .415 then must become 41¢.

Would you get the same results by adding the tax to each item as you placed it in the basket?

KEYS TO HOME MANAGEMENT
Keys to Comparative Shopping

Like most of us, you're probably interested in getting the most for your money. One easy way to compare items and check which is really the best buy is to compare the *unit* price of each. The item with the lowest unit price is most economical. To find the unit price of any item, just divide the item's cost by the number of units contained.

Here's an example: You're buying laundry detergents, and you're confronted with a shelf full of (essentially) the same product in boxes labeled with different weights and prices. Which is the best buy?

Box a) $8.83 / 9,072 grams
    b) $4.68 / 4,848 grams   (assume each requires the
    c) $3.96 / 4,451 grams   same amount of product
    d) $2.35 / 2,381 grams   per washer load.)

Equation: Cost ÷ units = cost per unit (or, in this case, since units are so small, it may be easier to figure cost per hundred units: (Cost ÷ units) × 100 = cost per 100 gms.)

Press   **Display/Comments**

8.83 ÷ 9,072 × 100 = **.09733245**   cost of *a* per 100 grams
4.68 ÷ 4,848 × 100 = **.09653465**   cost of *b* per 100 grams
3.96 ÷ 4,451 × 100 = **.08896877**   cost of *c* per 100 grams
2.35 ÷ 2,381 × 100 = **.09869803**   cost of *d* per 100 grams

So, "c" is the least expensive and the best buy, "d" is the most expensive.

When buying detergents, it's a good idea to keep in mind other important considerations such as which brands are biodegradeable, and which may require less product per wash load.

Buying by Area — Paint, Fertilizer, etc.

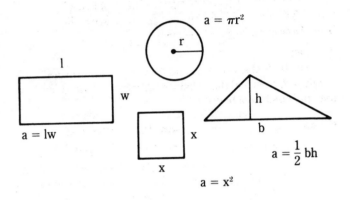

$$a = \pi r^2$$

$$a = lw$$

$$a = x^2$$

$$a = \frac{1}{2} bh$$

The need for some quick calculations can arise when you're buying a can of paint, a bag of fertilizer, or anything designed to be spread over an area. Your calculator can help you to be sure you've bought the right amount. (With the metric system coming in keep an eye on the various area units that will be in use.)

Example:
You have to put two coats of paint on 4 walls, each 10 feet high by 22 feet wide. One can of paint covers 400 square feet (1 coat). Paint costs $8.10 per can. Find the total cost.

Press	**Display/Comments**
10 ☒ 22 ☒ 4 ⊜	**880.** square feet of wall area
☒ 2 ⊜	**1760.** square feet for 2 coats
⊕ 400	Divide by the number of square feet covered with 1 can
⊜	**4.4** cans. (You'd have to buy 5 cans)
5 ☒ 8.10 ⊜	**40.5** Total job cost $40.50

Here's another one:

You have the happy chore of fertilizing a 100 by 100 meter lawn. The fertilizer you're using should be applied at a rate of 5 lbs per 1000 square feet, and comes in 50 lb bags. How many bags do you need?

Solution:

One way to do this is to first find the area of the lawn in *square feet;* then find the amount of fertilizer you need, and then the number of bags:

Press

100 ⊠ 3.28 ⊟ x^2

⊞ 1000 ⊠ 5 ⊟

⊞ 50 ⊟

Display/Comments

107584. This is the area of your lawn in square feet. Then:
537.92 This is the number of pounds you need. Finally,
10.7584 So, the number of bags you would need is 11.

Buying by Length —
Fence, Curtains, etc.

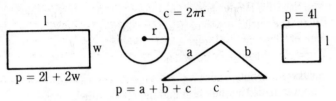

$p = 2l + 2w$ $c = 2\pi r$ $p = a + b + c$ $p = 4l$

If you have to figure the total cost of fence, curtains, or
other such items, just be sure to find the total length and
multiply by the cost per unit length (be sure the units
of length are the same before you multiply).

Example:
A rectangular field is 40 meters on one side and 60 meters on
the other. You want to fence its perimeter with fence that
costs $2.50 per foot. What is the total cost?

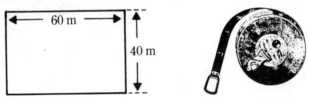

Solution: First, find the field perimeter:

Press	**Display/Comments**
(2 × 40) + (2 × 60) =	**200.** This is the field perimeter in meters. Now convert to feet:
× 3.28 =	**656.** and multiply by the cost per foot
× 2.50 =	**1640.** (a big job!)

With the metric system now being adopted, you'll be
seeing a lot of problems like this one with "mixed"
metric and English units. Your calculator and this book (*Keying Up Conversions* section and *Appendix*) will make handling
these problems much easier.

KEYS TO HOME MANAGEMENT
Buying by Volume — Concrete, Sand, etc.

Before ordering trucks to deliver large loads of rather bulky stuff, your calculator can be a big help. Some simple calculations can make sure you don't wind up storing extra material, or paying for extra deliveries if you run short!

Items bought in bulk — such as concrete, sand, crushed stone, etc. are often sold by the cubic yard or "yard".

Example:
You're helping to put in a patio that'll be 6 inches thick, 12 feet wide and 20 feet long. Instead of mixing the concrete yourself, you're thinking that you'll buy it premixed, if you can do the whole job for less than $100. The best price you can find is $36 per cubic yard. Will $100 be enough?

Press	**Display/Comments**
	First — Find the volume of the patio:
0.5 ☒ 12 ☒ 20 ▭	**120.** Patio volume in cubic feet. Next, divide by the number of cubic feet in a cubic yard:
⊞ 27 ▭	**4.4444444** You'll need this many cubic yards.
	The cost:
☒ 36 ▭	**160.** $100 is not enough by a long shot. (Start mixing.)

Formulas to help you find the volume of common shapes you may find yourself "filling up" are in the appendix.

Keys to Calculating Series Discounts

The ⟨%⟩ key on your calculator handles add on or discount percentages with ease — it keeps track of intermediate results for you and lets you get instant answers when "bargaining".

Here's an example:
You buy a motorcycle direct from the factory. Catalog list price is $750.00. A series of discounts are offered on the bike: 25% (factory discount), 10% (employees' discount), and 5% (racer's discount). Calculate the invoice price you will pay, assuming that each discount, in order, is taken from the previous total and not from the list price.

Here's the series of calculations:
$$750 - 25\% \,(750) = \text{Price}_1$$
$$\text{Price}_1 - 10\% \,(\text{Price}_1) = \text{Price}_2$$
$$\text{Price}_2 - 5\% \,(\text{Price}_2) = \text{Price}_3$$

On your calculator:

Press	Display/Comments
750 ⟨−⟩ ⟨(⟩ 750 ⟨×⟩ .25 ⟨)⟩	**187.5** = Discount at 25%
⟨=⟩	**562.5** (Price$_1$)
⟨−⟩ ⟨(⟩ 562.5 ⟨×⟩ .10 ⟨)⟩	**56.25** = Discount at 10%
⟨=⟩	**506.25** (Price$_2$)
⟨−⟩ ⟨(⟩ 506.25 ⟨×⟩ .05 ⟨)⟩	**25.3125** = Discount at 5%
⟨=⟩	**480.9375** Final price: $480.94

What would the cost be if these discounts were all taken from the $750 list price?
Answer: $450.

KEYS TO HOME MANAGEMENT
Gas Mileage

On a full tank of gas, you drove 350 miles home from the beach before refilling. To fill the gas tank, it took 12.5 gallons of gas. During the next week, you drove a total of 225 miles in the city, and when you stopped for gas, the car took 9.5 gallons. What gas mileage, highway and city, is your car getting?

Equation: Miles ÷ gallons = miles per gallon (mpg)

Press   **Display/Comments**

350 ÷ 12.5 =   **28.**   mpg (highway)
225 ÷ 9.5 =   **23.684211**   mpg (city)

With the advent of the metric system we'll be buying liters of gas and driving kilometers of distance, so keep in mind that:

Miles per Gallon ✗ 0.4251 = Kilometers per Liter
Kilometers per Liter ✗ 2.352 = Miles per Gallon
Miles per Hour ✗ 1.609 = Kilometers per Hour
Kilometers per Hour ✗ 0.6214 = Miles per Hour

If your car averages 13.2 km/l, how many miles/gal. does it achieve?

Press   **Display/Comments**

13.2 ✗ 2.352 =   **31.0464**   mpg

Keys to Mortgage Calculations

One area where your calculator will be invaluable is in calculations involving mortgages and long term payments. Usually you'd have to wade through tables to check out alternatives for yourself. With your calculator, and the step-by-step procedure shown below, you're in control!

For example:
What is the difference in monthly payments between a 9% loan and an 8% loan on a $30,000., thirty-year house mortgage?

Formula: $PMT = B \div \left[\dfrac{1 - (1 + i)^{-n}}{i} \right]$ Where PMT = monthly payment, B = Balance owed, n = number of payments, i = monthly interest $= \dfrac{8\%}{12}$ and $\dfrac{9\%}{12}$.

Equations: $P_1 = 30,000 \div \left[\dfrac{1 - \left(1 + \dfrac{8\%}{12}\right)^{-360}}{\dfrac{8\%}{12}} \right]$

$P_2 = 30,000 \div \left[\dfrac{1 - \left(1 + \dfrac{9\%}{12}\right)^{-360}}{\dfrac{9\%}{12}} \right]$

To work this problem following the rules of algebraic hierarchy, we have to rearrange the problem and work it "inside out".

Press   **Display/Comments**

1 $+$ $($ .08
$\div$ 12 $)$ $=$ **1.0066667** This is the value of
                                 the innermost term. Notice that
                                 the percentage is entered as a
                                 decimal.

y^x 360 $+/-$ $=$ **0.09144336** This completes the
                                 first term.

$+/-$ $+$ 1 $=$ **0.90855664** Change signs and
                                 add 1 to complete the numerator.

$\div$ $($ .08 $\div$ 12
$)$ $=$ **136.28350** Work the denominator
                                 and finish the terms inside the
                                 brackets.

$1/x$ $\times$ 30000   **220.12937** Taking the reciprocal
$=$ STO   and multiplying is the same as
                                 dividing 30000 by the term in the
                                 brackets.

                                 Monthly payment at 8% (P.) =
                                 $220.13

                                 Now you're doing the same
                                 calculation for a 9% loan.

1 $+$ $($ .09 $\div$ 12
$)$ $=$ y^x 360 $+/-$
$=$ $+/-$ $+$ 1 $=$ $\div$
$($ .09 $\div$ 12 $)$ $=$
$1/x$ $\times$ 30000 $=$ **241.38678**
                                 $P_2 = 241.39
$-$ RCL $=$ **21.257415** $P_2 - P_1 = 21.26
                                 savings in monthly payment.

KEYS TO HOME MANAGEMENT
Keys to Saving Energy (and Money)

Suppose that you have one light in your apartment that you like to leave on all of the time. The lightbulb in it is a 100-watt bulb. If the power company rate is approximately 4¢ per kilowatt-hour, how much does that one light cost you over a period of 30 days? NOTE: A kilowatt-hour is 1,000 watts for one hour. How much would you save by changing the bulb to a 60-watt bulb?

Equations: Bulb wattage ÷ 1,000 × cost per kilowatt hour = cost for that light for one hour.
Cost for one hour × hours in day × days = cost for light for any number of days.

Press	Display/Comments	
100 ÷ 1,000 × .04 =	**0.004**	Cost for 100-watt bulb on for one hour
× 24 =	**0.096**	Cost for one 100-watt bulb on for one day
× 30 = STO	**2.88**	Cost for one 100-watt bulb kept on for 30 days
60 ÷ 1,000 × .04 =	**0.0024**	Cost of 60-watt bulb on for one hour
× 24 × 30 =	**1.728**	Cost of 60-watt bulb on for 30 days
EXC − RCL =	**1.152**	(About $1.15 savings per month by changing to 60-watt bulb)

A water leak can also cost you money. It is estimated that, with a water pressure of 50 pounds, a leak through a hole the size of a straight pin will waste 5,100 gallons per month. A leak through a hole the size of a thin pencil lead can lose 29,100 gallons per month. And if the hole is the size of a b-b shot, you'll lose 108,000 gallons in one month. (If it's a hot water leak, you also lose the cost of heating the water.)

KEYS TO HOME MANAGEMENT
Truth-In-Lending

The Truth-In-Lending law demands that money lending institutions fully disclose the annual interest rate on loans.
The approximate rate can be found by the formula:

$$R = \frac{2NI}{P(n + 1)}$$

where N = number of payments per year, I = finance charge in dollars, P = principal, and n = number of scheduled installment payments.

Assume you make a loan for $5,000 for 36 months. If the payments are made monthly and are $162.50 each, what is the annual percentage rate?

$$N = 12 \quad P = 5000 \quad n = 36$$
$$I = 162.5 \times 36 - 5000$$
$$R = \frac{2 \times 12 \times (162.5 \times 36 - 5,000)}{(5,000 \times (36 + 1))}$$

Press

Display/Comments

2 ⊠ 12 ⊠
〔 162.5 ⊠ 36 ⊟ 5,000 〕 ÷   **20400.**   Numerator.
〔 5,000 ⊠ 〔 36 ⊞ 1 〕   Remember to put
〕   parentheses around the
          entire denominator.
☐=   **0.11027027**
      $R = 11\%$ annual
      percentage rate

The Federal Truth-In-Lending law requires a full disclosure
of annual interest rates. It ordinarily saves you from
having to figure it. But, if your case is not covered
by the law, the above formula is your own do-it-yourself
kit. Keep it handy.

KEYS TO HOME MANAGEMENT
Hauling
and Holding

You can use your calculator to help estimate weights for common objects and substances you handle. A very handy table containing "Weights of Common Substances" is included here to help you. Here are a few examples.

Your mom puts an aquarium 1 foot by 2 feet by 2.5 feet on the glass coffee table in the living room and starts filling it. Is this advisable?

Press	**Display/Comments**
	First find the volume of the aquarium:
1 $\boxed{\times}$ 2 $\boxed{\times}$ 2.5 $\boxed{=}$	**5.** cu ft
	Now, look up the weight of one cubic foot of water and multiply:
$\boxed{\times}$ 62.5 $\boxed{=}$	**312.5** lbs. (don't do it!)

Another example:
You have 2 "yards" (cubic yards) of sand delivered in the front yard of your house, and want to move it to the back yard. You know you can handle 150 lbs. at a time in your wheelbarrow. How many trips will it take?

Solution:
First, find the total volume of the sand delivered in cubic feet, then look up the weight of sand per cubic foot in the table and multiply. Finally divide by 150 lbs. per wheelbarrow trip, to find the number of trips.

Press	**Display/Comments**
2 $\boxed{\times}$ 27 $\boxed{\times}$ 90 $\boxed{=}$	**4860.** lbs. (approximate weight of delivered sand)
$\boxed{+}$ 150 $\boxed{=}$	**32.4** about 33 trips!

Weights of Common Substances

Substance	Approximate weight in pounds per cubic foot
Aluminum	162
Books	30 to 40
Brass	500 to 525
Brick, common	125
Charcoal	15 to 30
Clothing, firmly packed	10 to 15
Concrete	145
Copper	540 to 555
Cork	15
Earth, moist, loose	70 to 80
Gasoline, kerosene, etc.	45 to 50
Glass	160 to 180
Gold	1204
Ice	57
Iron, cast	450
Lead	710
Mud	110 to 130
Oils, vegetable or mineral	55 to 60
Sand	90 to 120
Silver	655
Snow, fresh fallen	5 to 12
Snow, wet and compacted	15 to 50
Steel	490
Stone, unbroken	160 (varies with type)
*Water	62.5
**Wood, hard	45
**Wood, soft	30

*Use the weight of water for all water-like substances, such as canned vegetables, fruit juice, beverages or milk.

**Varies widely with type and moisture content.

UNLOCKING ALGEBRA
Introduction

A whole spectrum of problems from nature, the business world, science (and required classes) involve algebra. Your calculator can really be a key that "unlocks" algebra for you. Why, you say? Well, many of the problems people have with algebra aren't really problems with algebra at all! They're problems with *arithmetic*. Trying to keep all the additions, squarings, multiplications and other things straight — right while you're trying to concentrate on the construction of an equation or the real "whys" of a problem — can be very tricky. That's where your calculator can be a real key. It'll keep tabs on the numbers — while you concentrate on the algebra.

The following examples cover a variety of algebraic situations, and show how some of the standard tools of algebra can be used with your calculator. We hope these examples will be just the beginning for you! Once you're a little freer of the number juggling — you may find algebra "unlocks" itself!

UNLOCKING ALGEBRA
Opening Up Expressions

Many "expressions" are just collections of numbers, operations and/or terms that can be evaluated to one final number. You will find your calculator to be a very powerful tool in evaluating such expressions, but be careful to enter the expression properly. The following examples have been carefully put together to show you the ropes.

A. Sums and differences

$$(12 - 3) - (-6 + 9) =$$

Press

⦗ 12 ⊟ 3 ⦘ ⊟ ⦗ 6 +/−
⊞ 9 ⦘ ⊟

Display/Comments

6. Note that negative numbers are entered by pressing +/− after the number is entered.

B. Products

$$\left(\frac{1}{2} + 3\right)\left(6 - \frac{3}{4}\right) =$$

Press

⦗ 1 ⊡ 2 ⊞ 3 ⦘ ☒ ⦗ 3
⊡ 4 +/− ⊞ 6 ⦘ ⊟

Display/Comments

18.375 Note: *You must provide the operation sign between the parentheses and rearrange the problem to follow the rules of algebra.*

C. Quotients

$$\frac{\frac{7}{8} - 2}{12 + 4 - 6} =$$

If you visualize this problem as

$$\left(\frac{7}{8} - 2\right) \div \left(12 + 4 - 6\right) =, \text{ then entry}$$

into the calculator will be simple.

Press	**Display/Comments**

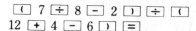

$$\boxed{(}\ 7\ \boxed{\div}\ 8\ \boxed{-}\ 2\ \boxed{)}\ \boxed{\div}\ \boxed{(}$$
$$12\ \boxed{+}\ 4\ \boxed{-}\ 6\ \boxed{)}\ \boxed{=}$$

−0.1125 Note: When more than one number is contained in the denominator, put parentheses around the whole thing.

D. Powers

$$\left(2 + \frac{3}{2} + \frac{1}{4}\right)^3 =$$

Press	**Display/Comments**

$$2\ \boxed{+}\ \boxed{(}\ 3\ \boxed{\div}\ 2\ \boxed{)}\ \boxed{+}\ \boxed{(}$$
$$1\ \boxed{\div}\ 4\ \boxed{)}\ \boxed{=}\ \boxed{y^x}\ 3\ \boxed{=}$$

52.734375 Caution: The $\boxed{y^x}$ operation will not handle a negative value for y. You'll have to keep track of the sign yourself when y is negative.

E. Mixed Operations

$$\frac{(6 \times (3-(9-5)^3))}{(2 + 6)\left(\dfrac{1}{2} - \dfrac{3}{4}\right)} =$$ (Good luck on this one!)

Press	**Display/Comments**

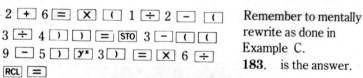

$$2\ \boxed{+}\ 6\ \boxed{=}\ \boxed{\times}\ \boxed{(}\ 1\ \boxed{\div}\ 2\ \boxed{-}\ \boxed{(}$$
$$3\ \boxed{\div}\ 4\ \boxed{)}\ \boxed{)}\ \boxed{=}\ \boxed{STO}\ 3\ \boxed{-}\ \boxed{(}\ \boxed{(}$$
$$9\ \boxed{-}\ 5\ \boxed{)}\ \boxed{y^x}\ 3\ \boxed{)}\ \boxed{=}\ \boxed{\times}\ 6\ \boxed{\div}$$
$$\boxed{RCL}\ \boxed{=}$$

Remember to mentally rewrite as done in Example C.
183. is the answer.

In this last example, keep two things in mind. First, the denominator contains lots of terms, so it should be solved first and stored in memory. Second, allow some time for your calculator to finish working between key strokes.

UNLOCKING ALGEBRA
Simplifying Expressions

Often in algebra you may be asked to *simplify* an expression. In these cases you are not given enough information to reduce the expression to a single number, but you can combine terms. For example:

Simplify the expression $13xy - 12x + 41y - 14(2x + y + 3xy)$.

Remember that terms containing x, xy, and y cannot be added or subtracted from each other unless the values of x and y are known. Since in this case such information is not provided, all you can do is simplify the expression by combining all the terms that contain x, y, or xy *separately*. (This process is called combining like terms.) Remember $a(b+c) = ab + ac$.

Press	**Display/Comments**
	First combine the terms containing x
14 +/– × 2 – 12 =	**–40.** x
	Then combine the xy terms
14 +/– × 3 + 13 =	**–29.** xy
	Then add the y terms
14 +/– × 1 + 41 =	**27.** y

The expression may be simplified to $-40x - 29xy + 27y$. It is accepted practice to write expressions of this sort in alphabetical order of the variables.

UNLOCKING ALGEBRA
Vocabulary of Simple Equations

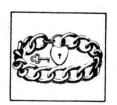

You'll find your calculator a big help in performing the arithmetic associated with equations—but *you* have to supply the algebra. In many algebra classes a lot of time will be spent solving simple equations, so it will be handy to know how your calculator can help.

Some special words are used when talking about equations. The equal sign is understood to separate the equation into two parts: a left side, and a right side. The numbers which multiply the unknowns are called *coefficients* and the other numbers in the equation are called *constants*.

Now look at the equation $3x = 18$. The method used to find the number represented by x is to divide both sides by 3.

$$\frac{3}{3}x = \frac{18}{3} \text{ or } 1x = \frac{18}{3} \text{ or } x = \frac{18}{3} \text{ (since 1x is just)}$$

written as x.) To solve with your calculator:

Press

18 ÷ 3 =

Display/Comments

6.   so x = 6

Now solve $3x + x = 11 - 6.3$

First combine all of the unknown terms on the left and then combine all of the constants on the right; the result will be a simple equation of the same form as the first example.

Press

3 + 1 = STO

11 − 6.3 =

÷ RCL =

Display/Comments

4. x   on the left side stored for later.
4.7   on the right side. At this point the equation has been simplified to $4x = 4.7$
1.175   You just divided both sides of the equation by 4. So, x = 1.175.

4-5

UNLOCKING ALGEBRA
Moving Terms in Simple Equations

Often in solving simple equations it will be necessary to move terms from one side of the equals sign to the other — to separate the known from the unknown terms. Your calculator will make things easier by keeping track of the arithmetic — you'll have to help it by keeping in mind some of the rules illustrated below.

Example:

Solve $4.2x - 16.3 = 6x - 7.6$ for x.

Solution: First, move the 6x term to the left side of the equation. This can be done by adding −6x to both sides. In this way the quantity 6x is removed from the right side and appears on the left side as −6x. (Many people just remember to change the sign of a term as it moves across the equal sign.) Next, the −16.3 needs to be moved to the right side, so add 16.3 to both sides. The −16.3 becomes +16.3 on the right side. To solve this equation with your calculator

Press

4.2 $\boxed{-}$ 6 $\boxed{=}$ $\boxed{\text{STO}}$

7.6 $\boxed{+/-}$ $\boxed{+}$ 16.3 $\boxed{=}$

$\boxed{\div}$ $\boxed{\text{RCL}}$ $\boxed{=}$

Display/Comments

−**1.8** x   on the left side stored for later

8.7   on the right side. The equation is now
−1.8x = 8.7

−**4.8333333**   You just divided both sides of the equation by −1.8,
x = −4.8333333.

Checking Your Results

A big advantage to solving equations using the calculator
is that checking your result is very easy. *You can always
know that you are right (or wrong).* Just store the value of
x in memory, and then use it to evaluate both sides of the
equation. If you have correctly solved the equation, the
left side should always equal the right side.

For example, in the previous equation the result was
x = −4.8333333. Store this value in memory. Now evaluate
both sides of the equation:

4.2x − 16.3 = 6x − 7.6, and use the recall key for x,
wherever it appears.

Press	**Display/Comments**
[STO] 4.2 [X] [RCL] [−] 16.3 [=]	**−36.6** Value of the right side. You need to record this value or remember it.
6 [X] [RCL] [−] 7.6 [=]	**−36.6** The equation is correctly solved since the two sides are equal.

Sometimes the value of the two sides will not be precisely
equal, even when the equation is solved properly, because
the calculator will "round off" numbers internally.

Simple Equations- Step-by-Step Procedure

Here are some steps to follow in using your calculator to help in solving simple equations.

Step 1. Combine all variable term coefficients on the left side of the equation and store in the memory. (Remember to change the sign of any value that you "take" from the right side of the equation and move to the left.)

Step 2. Combine all nonvariable terms on the right side of the equation. (Remember to change the sign on any value that you "take" from the left side and move to the right side.)

Step 3. Press ⌗÷ RCL ⌗= The number in the display is the correct value for x.

Step 4. To check, store your result in memory, and use it to separately evaluate the two sides of the equation.(Just press RCL when the value of x is to be inserted.)

Try this one:

Solve for x when $3(0.2x + 0.6) = 0.5x - 7$

In this problem be careful in handling the parentheses. They must be handled using the distributive law. Remember that $3(0.2x + 0.6)$ equals $3(0.2x) + 3(0.6)$ — so *both* of the numbers in parentheses are multiplied by 3. To solve this equation with your calculator:

Press

3 ⌧×⌧ 0.2 ⌧−⌧ 0.5 ⌧=⌧ STO

3 ⌧×⌧ 0.6 ⌧+/−⌧ ⌧−⌧ 7 ⌧=⌧

⌧÷⌧ RCL ⌧=⌧

To check:

STO

3 ⌧×⌧ ⌧(⌧ 0.2 ⌧×⌧ RCL ⌧+⌧ 0.6 ⌧)⌧ ⌧=⌧

0.5 ⌧×⌧ RCL ⌧−⌧ 7 ⌧=⌧

Display/Comments

0.1 Step 1. (Combine "x terms)

−8.8 Step 2. (Combine constant terms)

−88. Step 3. x = −88

Step 4. First store your result, and then use it to evaluate both sides of the equation.

−51. Value of the left side.

−51. Value of the right side. Solution correct.

UNLOCKING ALGEBRA
Equations, Fractions, and Your Calculator

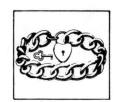

Equations with fractions may look tricky, but with your calculator helping you with accurate arithmetic (and a check on your results) you can handle them with little hassle. Here's an example which involves two sets of parentheses as well as fractions.

Solve for x when: $3.5 \left(\frac{1}{3}x - \frac{3}{5}\right) = \frac{3}{5}\left(2 - \frac{2}{9}x\right).$

Press

3.5 ⊠ 1 ÷ 3 ⊕ ⌈⌉ ⌈⌉ 3 ÷ 5
⌉ ⊠ ⌈⌉ 2 ÷ 9 ⌉ ⌉ ⊟
STO

3.5 ⊠ 3 ÷ 5 ⊕ ⌈⌉ 3 ÷ 5
⊠ 2 ⌉ ⊟

÷ RCL ⊟

To check:

STO

3.5 ⊠ ⌈⌉ 1 ÷ 3 ⊠
RCL ⊟ ⌈⌉ 3 ÷ 5 ⌉ ⌉ ⊟
3 ÷ 5 ⊠ ⌈⌉ 2 ⊟ ⌈⌉ 2 ÷
9 ⊠ RCL ⌉ ⌉ ⌉ ⊟

Display/Comments

1.3 This is the coefficient of x on the left side (Step 1)

3.3 Sum of constants on the right side (Step 2)
2.5384615 Value of x (Step 3)

Store your result, and evaluate both sides of the equation.
0.86153846 Value of left side.
0.86153846 Value of right side.
The solution is correct.

UNLOCKING ALGEBRA
Adding Equations
— Why? How?

Many problems, particularly word problems, will result in *two* linear equations which must then be solved for *two* unknowns. The following examples will introduce concepts that will be handy in solving such equations.

Example 1. Adding Equations.

One dollar is equivalent in value to 10 nickels and 2 quarters. A debt of 25¢ may be thought of as owing 5 nickels. You can express these two statements in "equation" form, and then add them as follows:

$$1 \text{ dollar} = 10 \text{ nickels} + 2 \text{ quarters}$$

plus $\underline{\quad -25¢ = -5 \text{ nickels} \qquad\qquad\qquad}$

$$1 \text{ dollar} - 25¢ = 10 \text{ nickels} + 2 \text{ quarters} - 5 \text{ nickels}$$

or $\qquad 100¢ - 25¢ = 50¢ + 50¢ - 25¢$

or $\qquad\qquad 75¢ = 75¢.$ 　　Notice that

it is correct to add two equations because you really are just adding equivalent quantities to each side of the first equation.

Example 2. Add the equations $3x + 4y = 7$, $2x - 3y = -5$

$$3x + 4y = 7$$

plus $\qquad \underline{2x - 3y = -5}$

$$3x + 4y + 2x - 3y = 7 - 5$$

Combining terms gives $5x + y = 2$. This equation was generated from the two previous equations using sound mathematics. This equation will have the same solutions for x and y as the original two equations.

Example 3. Add the equations $3x + 4y = 7$ and $-3x + 5y = 8$

$$3x + 4y = 7$$

plus $\underline{-3x + 5y = 8}$

$$9y = 15$$

When these two linear equations are added the result is a simple equation which can be solved for y. This value for y is the solution for y in the original equations. The x terms "vanished" when the equations were added. Think about this — can you always cause one of the unknowns to vanish when adding 2 equations?

(The answer is YES!) This procedure is illustrated in the next examples — and is the first step in solving *2 equations with 2 unknowns.*

4-10

UNLOCKING ALGEBRA
Adding Equations to Eliminate an Unknown

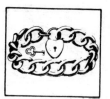

Example 1. Cause the x terms to vanish when adding the equations x + 3y = 7 and −2x + 2y = 3

One way to arrange for the x terms to vanish is to multiply both sides of the first equation by 2.

$$2(x + 3y) = 2(7)$$ Remember a(b + c) = ab + ac

so $$2x + 6y = 14$$ Now add this equation to the second

equation $$\underline{-2x + 2y = 3}$$
$$8y = 17$$ is the result. This equation could now be solved for y.

Example 2. Cause the x terms to vanish when adding the equations 4x + 3y = 3 and 3x + 4y = 6.

The trick is to make the x terms have equal values, but opposite signs. Focus on what is necessary to change *4x* to *−3x*. One way is to divide 4x by 4 leaving 1x, and then to multiply by −3. Dividing by 4 and multiplying by −3 is the same as multiplying by $-\frac{3}{4}$, so multiply both sides of the first equation by $-\frac{3}{4}$.

$$-\frac{3}{4}\left(4x + 3y\right) = -\frac{3}{4}\left(3\right)$$ which becomes: $$-3x - \frac{9}{4}y = -\frac{9}{4}$$

Now, adding the second equation:

$$\underline{3x + 4y = 6}$$
$$-\frac{9}{4}y + 4y = -\frac{9}{4} + 6$$

which can be further reduced to: $1.75y = 3.75$

The x terms vanished when the equations were added. The resulting equation may be solved for y. Adding equations to eliminate one of the variables is the first step in solving two simultaneous linear equations with 2 unknowns by the addition method.

UNLOCKING ALGEBRA
Solution of Two Linear Equations

The solution to many problems, both from algebra class and everyday life, often boils down to solving 2 equations with 2 unknowns. Your calculator will help by keeping track of the arithmetic — while you handle the algebra. (The previous 2 sections get together the facts you'll need.)

Example:
Find x and y when $x + y = 2$ and $2x - 3y = 5$.

Solution:
First, use the addition method to eliminate the x terms. In order for the x term in the first equation to equal the negative of the x term in the second equation, it should be multiplied by -2.

$$-2(x + y) = -2(2) \text{ or } -2x - 2y = -4$$

Now add this equation to the second equation
The result is

$$\begin{array}{r} 2x - 3y = 5 \\ \hline -5y = 1 \end{array}$$

This equation may be solved for y giving $y = -\dfrac{1}{5}$.

Now substitute this value of y back into the first equation and find x. In $x + y = 2$ if $y = -\dfrac{1}{5}$ then $x - \dfrac{1}{5} = 2$. On your calculator:

Press

2 $\boxed{+}$ $\boxed{(}$ 1 $\boxed{\div}$ 5 $\boxed{)}$ $\boxed{=}$

Display/Comments

2.2 This is the value of x, so $x = 2.2$ and $y = -\dfrac{1}{5}$.

Next check these values to make sure they also work in the second equation: $2x - 3y = 5$.

Does $2(2.2) - 3\left(-\dfrac{1}{5}\right) = 5$?

2 $\boxed{\times}$ 2.2 $\boxed{-}$ $\boxed{(}$ 3 $\boxed{\times}$ $\boxed{(}$ 1 $\boxed{+/-}$ $\boxed{\div}$
5 $\boxed{)}$ $\boxed{)}$ $\boxed{=}$

5. The equations are both true when $x = 2.2$ and $y = -\dfrac{1}{5}$.

4-12

Solution of an Investment Problem

Ms. Johnson would like to invest her savings of $20,500 in both government bonds paying 5.5% interest and stock which she expects to pay 8% interest. She would like an income from her investment of $120 per month. Let B represent the amount to be invested in bonds and S represent the amount to be invested in stock.

$$B + S = 20,500 \text{ dollars} \quad \text{(total amount)}$$
and $$0.055B + 0.08S = 120(12) \quad \text{(yearly income)}$$

The first equation can be multiplied by −0.055 and then added to the second equation to remove the B terms.

$$-0.055 (B + S) = -0.055 (20,500)$$

Press | **Display/Comments**

0.055 +/− ☒ 20,500 ═ | **−1127.5**
So the first equation becomes: | −0.055B − 0.055S = −1127.5
adding the second equation to it | <u>0.055B + 0.08 S = 120(12)</u>

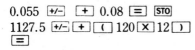

Press | **Display/Comments**

0.055 +/− ＋ 0.08 ═ STO | **0.025** the coefficient of S
1127.5 +/− ＋ ⬅ 120 ☒ 12 ➡ |
═ | **312.5** So, adding the two
| equations gives:
To finish the solution for S: | 0.025S = 312.5
÷ RCL ═ | **12500.** dollars to be
| invested in stock (S).

To find the amount to be invested in bonds substitute 12500 for S in the first equation: B + 12500 = 20,500

Press | **Display/Comments**
20500 ⊟ 12500 ═ | **8000.** dollars to be
| invested in bonds (B).

Now, check in the second equation, substituting for B and S
$$0.055 (8000) + 0.08 (12500) = 120(12)$$

Press | **Display/Comments**

.055 ☒ 8000 ＋ ⬅ 0.08 ☒ |
12500 ➡ ═ | **1440.**
120 ☒ 12 ═ | **1440.** The solutions are
| correct. **4**-13

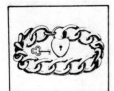

UNLOCKING ALGEBRA
Linear Equations with Fractions

With your calculator helping to handle the arithmetic, even equations involving fractions can be tackled with much less chance for error. *For example:*

Find x and y when $\frac{2}{3}x - \frac{4}{5}y = -1.2$ and $\frac{4}{5}x + 2y = 10.4$

First, change the x term in the first equation so that it equals the negative of the x term in the second equation.

To find the equalizing factor, divide *the coefficient* you want $(-4/5)$ by *the present coefficient* $(2/3)$. Then multiply each term in the equation by the result. (This method always works!)

Press

4 +/- ÷ 5 ÷ (2 ÷ 3)
= STO

2 ÷ 3 X RCL =
4 +/- ÷ 5 X RCL =
1.2 +/- X RCL =

Next, add the second equation

0.8 +/- + (4 ÷ 5) =

0.96 + 2 = STO

1.44 + 10.4 =

÷ RCL =

Display/Comments

−1.2 Use this number to multiply the first equation.
−0.8x
0.96y
1.44
The first equation is now $-0.8x + 0.96y = 1.44$

$$\frac{4}{5}x + \quad 2y = 10.4$$

0. as desired — the x term has vanished.
2.96 y. (y is now the only variable.)
11.84

4. so y = 4

Substitute this value of y into the first equation to find x. Solve

$$\frac{2}{3}x - \frac{4}{5}(4) = -1.2$$

1.2 +/- + (4 ÷ 5 X 4) =
÷ (2 ÷ 3) =   **3.** so $x = 3$.

Now check in the second equation:

4 ÷ 5 X 3 + (2 X 4) = **10.4**   which is correct.

UNLOCKING ALGEBRA
Scientific Notation

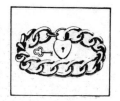

Handling very large and very small numbers becomes a snap on your calculator. This enables you to ponder on some pretty wild things! *For example:*

If one piece of paper is 10^{-4}m thick, how many pieces of paper piled flat will it take to make a pile as high as the moon? (The distance to the moon is about 3.8×10^8m.)

Solution: The distance to the moon (d) equals the number of pages (n) times the thickness per page (t) so:

$$d = nt$$

or

$$n = \frac{d}{t}$$

$$n = \frac{3.8 \times 10^8 m}{10^{-4} m}$$

Note:

10^{-4} must be entered into the calculator as 1×10^{-4} if scientific notation is used.

Press

3.8 [EE↓] 8 [÷] 1 [EE↓] 4 [+/−] [=]

Display/Comments

3.8   12   The number of sheets is 3.8×10^{12}, or $3,800,000,000,000$.

Think about this one: If all of the people in a city with a population of 1 million had a 4-inch thick phone book, and they stacked them all up, how high would they go?

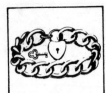

UNLOCKING ALGEBRA
Paper Pythagorean Theorem

Many years ago, a sharp man named Pythagoras developed a formula which is now often referred to as the Pythagorean theorem:

$$c^2 = a^2 + b^2$$

This equation applies to all *right triangles*. Since right triangles are pretty common things, the Pythagorean theorem is a very useful little formula. It basically states that no matter how a right triangle is constructed, the square of the longest side equals the sum of the squares of the other two sides. You might like to see this for yourself.

Try this—take a sheet of paper and use a corner as the right angle. Draw a straight line across the paper to form a triangle.

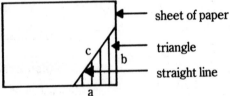

Here, c represents the length of the longest side (opposite the right angle), and a and b represent the length of the other two sides. With a ruler you can measure a, b, and c for yourself, and substitute your values into the formula $c^2 = a^2 + b^2$, to check it out.

You should find that the value you obtain for c^2 will be approximately (you can't measure the lengths exactly) the value obtained for $a^2 + b^2$.

Press

(your value for c) $\boxed{x^2}$

(your value for a) $\boxed{x^2}$ $\boxed{+}$

(your value for b) $\boxed{x^2}$ $\boxed{=}$

Display/Comments

Value for c^2

Value for $a^2 + b^2$
Are they equal?

The Pythagorean formula is used extensively in mathematics so make sure that you understand it.

UNLOCKING ALGEBRA
Examples of the Pythagorean Theorem

Example 1.

Suppose you have just purchased a tower for a radio antenna
which is 10 meters tall. You want to suspend the tower by
3 guy wires which will be located 6 meters from the base. How
much guy wire should you buy?

The tower and the distance along the ground to the guy
wires form right angles, so the Pythagorean
formula may be used.

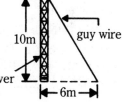

$$c^2 = a^2 + b^2$$
(length of guy wire)^2 = (height of tower)^2
+ (distance along the ground)^2
(length of guy wire)^2 = $10^2 + 6^2$
length of guy wire = $\sqrt{10^2 + 6^2}$

Press

10 $\boxed{x^2}$ $\boxed{+}$ 6 $\boxed{x^2}$ $\boxed{=}$ $\boxed{\sqrt{x}}$
$\boxed{\times}$ 3 $\boxed{=}$

Display/Comments

11.661904 length of 1 wire
34.985711 so you need
at least 35 meters of
guy wire for the 3
supports.

Example 2.

If your desk top is 75cm wide and 130cm long, how long is
a diagonal of the desk top?

Press

75 $\boxed{x^2}$ $\boxed{+}$ 130 $\boxed{x^2}$ $\boxed{=}$ $\boxed{\sqrt{x}}$

Display/Comments

150.08331 or about
150 cm

UNLOCKING ALGEBRA
Distance Between Two Points

Often, mathematics can be useful when calculating *distances*, whether it's navigating across an ocean, plotting points on a graph, or solving a problem in algebra class. A formula can be derived to help handle distance problems (often just called the "distance formula"). The distance formula is a special form of the Pythagorean theorem. Examine the examples shown below. They'll introduce some concepts used in deriving the distance formula — to show you how it works and where it came from.

Example 1. Two of your friends are walking away from you along a straight path. One friend walks 5 meters and the other walks 10 meters in the same direction. How far apart are your friends? (You probably can easily figure that the answer to this problem is 5 meters.) Examining a sketch of this problem:

$$\begin{array}{ccccccccccc} & & & & & \textbf{\textit{x}} & & & & & \textbf{\textit{x}} \\ \hline 0 & 1 & 2 & 3 & 4 & 5 & 6 & 7 & 8 & 9 & 10 \end{array} \quad \text{x direction}$$

Start $\qquad\qquad x_1 \qquad\qquad\qquad\quad x_2$

If you wanted to keep track of the direction your friends walked you could call it the x direction. You could represent the distance one friend walked as x_1, and the distance your other friend walked as x_2. Then you could write a formula for the distance they are apart: It would be $x_2 - x_1$. So the distance is $x_2 - x_1 = 10 - 5 = 5$ meters. Now suppose that one friend walks 3 meters in the opposite direction. Will the formula $x_2 - x_1$ still apply?

$$\begin{array}{cccccccccccccc} \textbf{\textit{x}} & & & & & & & & & & & & & \textbf{\textit{x}} \\ \hline -3 & -2 & -1 & 0 & 1 & 2 & 3 & 4 & 5 & 6 & 7 & 8 & 9 & 10 \end{array} \quad \text{x direction}$$

$x_1 \qquad\qquad\uparrow \qquad\qquad\qquad\qquad\qquad\qquad x_2$
Start

$x_2 - x_1 = 10 - (-3) = 13$ The formula still works!

(*Note:* If you reversed the order of this formula and found $x_1 - x_2$ you would get $(-3) - 10$ equals -13. This is the same distance, but is negative. As you'll see, when using the distance formula this is no problem since all distances are squared, and $(-13)^2 = 13^2$.)

4-18

Graphing, Distance, Pythagorean Theorem

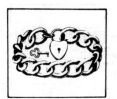

Graph the points (6,2) and (3,5) and find the distance between the two points (the length of line segment labeled "c" in the diagram). Use the Pythagorean theorem.

By looking at the graph, you can see that the length of side b is $6 - 3$, and the length of side a is $5 - 2$. Inserting these lengths into the Pythagorean formula gives $c^2 = (6 - 3)^2 + (5 - 2)^2$

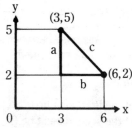

Press

(6 − 3) x^2 +
(5 − 2) x^2 = $\sqrt{x}$

Display/Comments

4.2426407 The points are about 4.2 units apart.

If you think about this example, you'll begin to see that a general formula for the distance between two points may be found as follows. Find the distance between the points (x_1, y_1) and (x_2, y_2), on the diagram below, using the Pythagorean formula.

$$d^2 = a^2 + b^2.$$

Looking at the graph you can see that the distance $a = (y_2 - y_1)$ and the distance $b = (x_2 - x_1)$, so

$$d^2 = (y_2 - y_1)^2 + (x_2 - x_1)^2$$

Take the positive square root of both sides of this equation and you'll get:

$$d = \sqrt{(y_2 - y_1)^2 + (x_2 - x_1)^2}$$

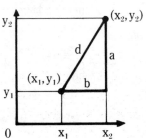

This useful result is often called the distance formula.

UNLOCKING ALGEBRA
Use of the
Distance Formula

Here are a few examples of how the distance formula (derived in the previous section) can come in handy. Your calculator makes using the formula quite easy.

Example 1.

Find the distance between these two graphed points: (6, 34) and (80, 37), using the distance formula.

Solution:

Let the first point be (x_1, y_1) so $x_1 = 6$ and $y_1 = 34$
Let the second point be (x_2, y_2) so $x_2 = 80$ and $y_2 = 37$
The distance formula is:

$$d = \sqrt{(y_2 - y_1)^2 + (x_2 - x_1)^2}\,.$$

Substitute in the values for x_1, x_2, y_1, and y_2.

$$d = \sqrt{(37 - 34)^2 + (80 - 6)^2}$$

Press   **Display/Comments**

(37 − 34) x^2 +
(80 − 6) x^2 = √ **74.060786**   The points are
                                              about 74 units apart.

Example 2.

Find the distance from (−6, 34) to (−30, 78). Notice that this problem involves negative numbers, so be careful when substituting them into the distance formula.

Solution:

Let the first point be (x_1, y_1) so $x_1 = -6$ and $y_1 = 34$
Let the second point be (x_2, y_2) so $x_2 = -30$ and $y_2 = 78$

$$d = \sqrt{(y_2 - y_1)^2 + (x_2 - x_1)^2}$$

$$d = \sqrt{(78 - 34)^2 + (-30 - (-6))^2}$$

Press   **Display/Comments**

(78 − 34) x^2 +
(30 +/− − 6 +/−)
x^2 = √   **56.850682**   These points are
                                              about 57 units apart.

UNLOCKING ALGEBRA
Factoring a Quadratic Equation

There are a variety of problems in nature that involve equations which contain both an x^2 and an x term (these are called quadratic equations). Solving these equations requires some special techniques which your calculator can make easier to handle and check on. For instance, solve for x when
$$x^2 + 5x + 6 = 0.$$

One technique for solving equations of this type is called *factoring*. This technique is based on a law from algebra called the distributive law. A special form of this law tells you that $(a + b)(c + d) = a(c + d) + b(c + d) = ac + ad + bc + bd$. This type of multiplication process is important in algebra and in handling quadratic problems — it's a good idea to get familiar with it. (You can substitute numbers into this and check it with your calculator if you have difficulty believing it.)

Now using this rule try multiplying $(x + 2)(x + 3)$. You should get $x^2 + 3x + 2x + 6$, which is equal to $x^2 + 5x + 6$. Compare this to the original equation.

Looking at the original equation $x^2 + 5x + 6 = 0$, it is now apparent that this equation may be written as
$$(x + 2)(x + 3) = 0$$
For this equation to be true, either the $(x + 2)$ or the $(x + 3)$ must equal 0. (Remember that any number times 0 is 0.) When $x + 2 = 0$, adding -2 to both sides gives $x = -2$; and when $x + 3 = 0$, adding -3 to both sides gives $x = -3$. So $x^2 + 5x + 6 = 0$ when $x = -2$ or $x = -3$. These are the two solutions or "roots" of the quadratic equation. Check by substitution.

Press	Display/Comments
2 [+/−] [x²] [+] [(] 5 [×] 2 [+/−] [)] [+] 6 [=]	**0.** So $x^2 + 5x + 6 = 0$ when $x = -2$.
3 [+/−] [x²] [+] [(] 5 [×] 3 [+/−] [)] [+] 6 [=]	**0.** So $x^2 + 5x + 6 = 0$ when $x = -3$.

The solutions to the original equation are $x = -2$ and $x = -3$.

UNLOCKING ALGEBRA
Derivation of the
Quadratic Formula

There is an important formula in algebra which allows you to solve even tough quadratic equations fairly easily especially with your calculator handling the arithmetic. A look at an example will help show how this formula came about:

Example:

Find x when $3x^2 + 2x - 15 = 0$
(You can try all day to factor this equation and it won't do much good.) There is another method of solving these equations which is called "completing the square." Completing the square is a lot of work though, so it is generally done for a generalized form of the equation. The resulting formula for the values of x is called the quadratic formula. The following is a "tour" of the steps it takes to cook up the quadratic formula.

The generalized form of a quadratic equation is $ax^2 + bx + c = 0$. All quadratic equations may be written in this form.

Divide both sides of the equation by a, giving $x^2 + \dfrac{b}{a}x + \dfrac{c}{a} = 0$.

Add $\dfrac{b^2}{4a^2} - \dfrac{c}{a}$ to both sides giving $x^2 + \dfrac{b}{a}x + \dfrac{b^2}{4a^2} = \dfrac{b^2}{4a^2} - \dfrac{c}{a}$

Now the left side of the equation may be factored to give you:

$$\left(x + \frac{b}{2a}\right)^2 = \frac{b^2}{4a^2} - \frac{c}{a}$$

Taking the square root of both sides of the equation gives

$$x + \frac{b}{2a} = \pm \sqrt{\frac{b^2}{4a^2} - \frac{c}{a}}$$

Now adding $-\dfrac{b}{2a}$ to both sides gives $x = -\dfrac{b}{2a} \pm \sqrt{\dfrac{b^2}{4a^2} - \dfrac{c}{a}}$

The general equation has now been solved for x. This equation is normally written in another form for ease of calculation, as we'll now show.

Multiply the $-\dfrac{c}{a}$ term by $\dfrac{4a}{4a}$ giving $x = -\dfrac{b}{2a} \pm \sqrt{\dfrac{b^2}{4a^2} - \dfrac{4ac}{4a^2}}$.

Add the terms under the radical: $x = -\dfrac{b}{2a} \pm \sqrt{\dfrac{b^2 - 4ac}{4a^2}}$.

Remember $\sqrt{\dfrac{d}{e}} = \dfrac{\sqrt{d}}{\sqrt{e}}$, so $x = -\dfrac{b}{2a} \pm \dfrac{\sqrt{b^2 - 4ac}}{2a}$

Adding gives the accepted form of the quadratic formula:

$$x = \frac{-b \pm \sqrt{b^2 - 4ac}}{2a}$$

UNLOCKING ALGEBRA
Using the Quadratic Formula

The quadratic formula (derived in the previous section) may look tricky to evaluate — but with your calculator handling the squares, square roots and keeping accurate track of what's going on, it's much less hassle.

Example:
Find the values of x which satisfy the equation $3x^2 + 2x - 15 = 0$. This is a quadratic equation written in the form $ax^2 + bx + c = 0$. The values of a, b and c are $a = 3$, $b = 2$ and $c = -15$. Substituting these values into the quadratic formula:

$$x = \frac{-b \pm \sqrt{b^2 - 4ac}}{2a}$$ gives values for x of

$$\frac{-2 + \sqrt{2^2 - 4(3)(-15)}}{2(3)} \text{ and } \frac{-2 - \sqrt{2^2 - 4(3)(-15)}}{2(3)}$$

Since the radical term is the same in these two solutions, it will be evaluated first.

Press	**Display/Comments**
2 $\boxed{x^2}$ $\boxed{-}$ $\boxed{(}$ 4 $\boxed{\times}$ 3 $\boxed{\times}$ 15 $\boxed{+/-}$	
$\boxed{)}$ $\boxed{=}$ $\boxed{\sqrt{x}}$ $\boxed{STO}$	**13.56466**
	Value of the radical term now stored for later use.
2 $\boxed{+/-}$ $\boxed{+}$ $\boxed{RCL}$ $\boxed{=}$ $\boxed{\div}$ $\boxed{(}$ 2	One solution is x =
$\boxed{\times}$ 3 $\boxed{)}$ $\boxed{=}$	**1.9274433**
2 $\boxed{+/-}$ $\boxed{-}$ $\boxed{RCL}$ $\boxed{=}$ $\boxed{\div}$ $\boxed{(}$ 2	Another solution is x =
$\boxed{\times}$ 3 $\boxed{)}$ $\boxed{=}$	**−2.59411** (Store it for checking)

These values may be checked in the original equation.

UNLOCKING ALGEBRA
Graphing, Roots of a Polynomial

Graphs of equations are often intriguing (and sometimes beautiful) pictures that show how functions work. They can be used in tackling some solutions that might otherwise be next to impossible. Your calculator makes graphing much easier than ever before. *For example:*

Find the values of x which are solutions (roots) of the equation.

$$x^4 - 14x^3 + 63x^2 - 106x + 56 = 0$$

This is a polynomial equation, and these are normally very difficult to solve, but your calculator will greatly reduce the difficulty. Polynomials often have several roots and the easiest method of solution may be to assume that the equation equals y and graph it. *The points where the curve crosses the x axis are roots* (where the polynomial equals zero).

Evaluate the polynomial when x = 3.

Display/Comments

Press

3 [STO]

Store the value of x since it will be needed several times.

[Yˣ] 4 [−] [(] 14 [×] [(] [RCL] [Yˣ] 3 [)] [)] [+] [(] 63 [×] [RCL] [x²] [)] [−] [(] 106 [×] [RCL] [)] [+] 56 [=]

8.0000005 When x equals 3, y equals approximately 8.

As many points as needed may be evaluated with your calculator.

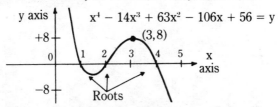

Note: This method will not work to find negative roots unless you keep track of the signs mentally, since [Yˣ] cannot be used with a negative value for y.
Also, remember to allow some time for your calculator to "think" between keystrokes — particularly when using the [Yˣ] key.

WALL STREET

TURNING TO BUSINESS AND FINANCE
Introduction

Until now, the math for your major financial decisions may have been "handled" by others — you've had to take your lumps "trusting" someone else's calculations. But now, using your calculator, you can personally check the weird-looking formulas and calculations related to finances. Even *interest* problems are easy with the help of the y^x key.

The examples in this section will not only illustrate the y^x key, but will also show with some everyday examples how your calculator can help you check financial math and assist you in making money-saving decisions.

TURNING TO BUSINESS AND FINANCE
Figuring Points

When selling a house, you often have to "pay real estate points". This means that due to differences in interest rates the *seller* has to pay extra interest (called points) on a house that is refinanced through FHA. Real estate points are often charged on the basis of *4 points for each 1% difference in interest rates between the FHA or VA loan and the conventional bank-type loan.*

As an example, consider that you're selling a house for $28,000 through an FHA loan with 4% down (you don't pay points on the down payment) and at a 9% interest rate on the balance. Let's say that the conventional loan rate on the same amount is 9¾% interest. On this basis,
a) How many points do you as seller have to pay? and
b) How much money do these points represent? (*Each point represents 1% of the selling price less the down payment.*)

Solution:
a) Number of points = (9¾ − 9) × 4
   (Note 9¾ = 9.75)

b) Cost of points = (28,000 − 4 [%]) × (# of points [%])

Press   **Display/Comments**

a)
  [(] 9.75 [−] 9 [)]
  [×] 4 [=]   **3.**   points
b)
28000 [STO] [×] .04 [=] [+/−]
    [+] [RCL] [=] [×] .03 [=] **806.4**   cost of points

The "point" system is part of the settlement cost to the seller of real estate. However, in anticipation of this cost, the seller usually prices the property higher. The result is that points effectively increase the interest rate on the loan to the buyer.

Foreign Travel Money Mixup

Someday we all want to take an international trip. When you do, though, one item will be of central importance — your money. You're concerned not only with the money you start with, but also how much your money is worth in another country's currency. For example, if you're quoted foreign prices for various expenses of hotel, entertainment, etc., you need to know how much money to take. To do this, you have to know the value of the U.S. dollar with respect to the currency of the country you're going to visit.

For example, the imaginary country of Xero has a monetary exchange rate such that one dollar equals 1.3 Z's (the Z is their unit of currency). O.K., you know your total expenses will be $351 for air fare, 2413 Z's for hotel, guide, and entertainment, and $672 for a return boat trip (including miscellaneous expenses).

a) How much money in dollars will you need for the trip?

b) You saved 200 Z's as souvenirs. But, on your boat trip, you needed the extra cash at one of the island stops. If the island's currency, the KO, has an exchange rate of 0.79 KO's to one U.S. dollar, how many KO's did you get for the 200 Z's?

Solution:

a) To solve, first convert the Z's to dollars and then add the dollar amounts together for the total. Since 1.3 Z's = $1, the conversion factor $1 = \left(\dfrac{\$1}{1.3Z}\right)$ is used.

Total dollars = $351 + (2413 \ Z) \left(\dfrac{\$1}{1.3Z}\right) + \$672$

b) Since 1.3 Z = $1 and 0.79 KO = $1, 1.3 Z's = 0.79 KO. This means that $\dfrac{0.79 \ KO}{1.3 \ Z}$ is the conversion factor.

Total KO's = $200 \ Z's \times \left(\dfrac{0.79 \ KO}{1.3 \ Z}\right)$

Press	**Display/Comments**	
a) 351 $+$	**351.**	
$($ 2413 $\times$ 1 $\div$ 1.3 $)$	**1856.1538**	(This is the number of dollars in 2413 Z's.)
$-$ 672 $=$	**2879.1538**	Total dollars
b) 200 $\times$ .79 $\div$ 1.3 $=$	**121.53846**	Number of KO's

5-3

TURNING TO BUSINESS AND FINANCE
Foreign Travel
Devaluation

The value of the U.S. dollar varies throughout the world as the world economy fluctuates. A particularly important aspect of this can affect you if you're travelling in a country that *devaluates* its currency while you're there. Basically, devaluation means that a country changes its rate of currency exchange such that its currency is worth less (devaluated) with respect to other world monies.

For example, consider the country of Randia with its currency (the Rand) valued at 0.71 Rand for $1.00 (American). Assume that you traveled into Randia with $824 and transferred all of this money into the Rand (R).

a) How much money in Rands did you receive?

Now, during your visit in Randia, you spent 319 Rands and, before leaving, you returned to exchange the remainder of the money back into dollars. However, the Rand had just been *devalued* by the local government to 0.85 Rand per American dollar.

b) How much money in dollars did you receive after the devaluation?
c) If you had exchanged your money back to dollars before the devaluation, how many dollars would you have received?
d) How much money (American dollars) did you lose as a result of the devaluation?

Solution:

a) # of Rands you receive = ($824) $\left(\dfrac{0.71R}{\$1}\right)$ = a

b) Dollars you receive back after devaluation:
$$= (a - 319 \text{ R}) \left(\frac{\$1}{0.85R}\right) = b$$

c) Dollars you would have received back before devaluation = $(a - 319 \text{ R}) \left(\dfrac{\$1}{0.71R}\right)$ = c

d) Money you lost = c − b

Press	Display/Comments

a)
824 $\boxed{\times}$ .71 $\boxed{=}$ $\boxed{STO}$ **585.04**   Rands now stored for next step.

b)
$\boxed{(}$ $\boxed{RCL}$ $\boxed{-}$ 319 $\boxed{)}$
$\boxed{STO}$ **266.04**   (a − 319) stored for c below.
$\boxed{\div}$ 0.85 $\boxed{=}$ **312.98824** or $312.99 dollars received

c)
$\boxed{RCL}$ $\boxed{\div}$ .71 $\boxed{=}$ **374.70423** or $374.70 you would have received before devaluation.

d)
$\boxed{-}$ 312.98824 $\boxed{=}$ **$61.71599** loss

Devaluation of money can spell *sudden loss* for international tourists or merchants. Devaluation of money spells *bankruptcy* for governments which practice it too much and too often.

TURNING TO BUSINESS AND FINANCE
Buying a Car
Early Payoff

You've just received a nice raise and it's time to buy a new car. However, you're still making payments on your present car. Before you go shopping for a new car, you need to determine how much you have left to pay off on your old car, so you can determine how much of the trade-in offer will be left toward the down payment on the new one.

As a guess on the amount you still owe on your old car, you can take the number of remaining payments times your monthly payment. This actually is too large a figure, though, since it also includes the interest you're paying. To get the exact figure you need to use this formula:

$$\text{Bal} = \text{Pmt} \left[\frac{1 - (1 + i)^{k-n}}{i} \right] \text{ where}$$

Bal = Payoff balance
Pmt = current monthly payment
i   = monthly interest rate or the $\left(\frac{\text{annual rate}}{12} \right)$
k   = number of payments already made, and
n   = total number of monthly payments.

This formula may look tricky; however, your calculator makes it easy. For example, say your original loan was for 36 months (n) and you've just made the 23rd payment (k) of $103.23. What's your payoff balance if the interest is 11.88% per year? $\left(\frac{11.88\%}{12} \right)$ = .99% per month.

Solution:

Press   **Display/Comments**

1 ⬛− ⬛(
⬛(1 ⬛+ .0099 ⬛)   **1.0099**
⬛y^x ⬛(23 ⬛− 36 ⬛) ⬛) ⬛=   **0.12020566** *Note:* After
pushing this second ⬛) wait for the calculator, as it takes some
time for this ⬛y^x calculation. Do not press the next key until the
⬛y^x calculation is finished.
⬛× 103.23 ⬛÷ .0099 ⬛=   **1253.4172** so the payoff
amount is $1253.42 (your loan company may charge extra for
early payoff, though).

Now, you know your payoff, you've shopped around, and you
fairly well know the price on your new car. However, you
want to check on what your new monthly payments will be.
This same formula will work if you rearrange it to this:

$$\text{Pmt} = \text{Bal} \div \left[\frac{1 - (1 + i)^{\,k-n}}{i} \right]$$

Find your new monthly payment using $k = 0$ (no payments yet),
36-month loan, 1% per month interest (12% per year) on a
principal of $4620.

Press   **Display/Comments**

1 ⬛− ⬛(⬛(1 ⬛+ .01 ⬛)   **1.01**
⬛y^x 36 ⬛+/− ⬛) ⬛=   **0.30107505**
Again, wait until the number in the display is completed
before proceeding. Also, notice the use of the ⬛+/− key to make
the 36 negative. This avoids using an extra ⬛(and
entering 0-36 since K is 0. (Note: Do not try to make the 36
negative by this sequence ⬛− 36 as this produces an error.)
⬛÷ .01 ⬛= ⬛STO 4620 ⬛÷ ⬛RCL ⬛=   **153.45011**   payment
                                                          per month

TURNING TO BUSINESS AND FINANCE
Interest on the Interest

Each of us should have some sort of plan for financial security for our future. This can include everything from gum ball banks to savings accounts, annuities, or even property and equipment for investments. Getting into various plans and understanding them can be a rather complex process at first glance. Some business math situations can seem to be an unreal maze of formulas involving long periods of interest, numbers raised to the 200th power and so on. Your calculator, however, can help make the math involved much more "doable" and understandable. Solving some of these problems can be almost impossible by conventional methods of logarithms and compound interest tables, etc. However, your calculator enables solutions that are striking examples of its outstanding labor-saving capabilities.

For example, consider regular deposits into an interest-bearing account, like a savings account. If you deposit $180 each month into an account that pays 6% annually, how much money would you have in 10 years?

Well, at first this doesn't seem too bad. You could just multiply the number of months in ten years by $180. But what about the interest? Then, after the first year, there's interest on the interest and so on...To get the exact amount after 10 years, all this may be figured by using the formula:

$$C = Pmt \left[\frac{(1 + i)^n - 1}{i} \right] \text{ where}$$

C = final "accrued" amount
Pmt = amount of regular payment
i = interest rate per deposit period (in this case $\frac{6\%}{12}$ or 0.5% per month)
n = total number of deposit periods (here $n = 12 \times 10$ or 120 months)

This formula can be worked using this set of keystrokes:

Pmt $\boxed{\times}$ $\boxed{(}$ $\boxed{(}$ 1 $\boxed{+}$ i $\boxed{\%}$ $\boxed{)}$ $\boxed{y^x}$ n $\boxed{-}$ 1
$\boxed{)}$ $\boxed{\div}$ i $\boxed{\%}$ $\boxed{=}$

Press | **Display/Comments**

180 $\boxed{\times}$ $\boxed{(}$ $\boxed{(}$ 1 $\boxed{+}$ .005
$\boxed{)}$ $\boxed{y^x}$ 120 $\boxed{-}$ 1$\boxed{)}$ **0.81939668**

$\boxed{\div}$ .005 $\boxed{=}$ **29498.28** total accrued amount
in 10 years.

How much would accrue after 2 years? The only thing changed
is n. For 2 years n = 12 × 2 or 24 .

Press | **Display/Comments**

180 $\boxed{\times}$ $\boxed{(}$ $\boxed{(}$ 1 $\boxed{+}$
.005 $\boxed{)}$ $\boxed{y^x}$ 24 $\boxed{-}$ 1$\boxed{)}$ **0.12715977**

$\boxed{\div}$ .005 $\boxed{=}$ **4577.7516**

WAKE UP, POOR FOLK!

~~100,000~~

EASY AND NOVEL WAYS

TO

MAKE MONEY.

Sure Guarantees, Ten Cents Each.

TURNING TO BUSINESS AND FINANCE
Marketable "Money"

When you think about savings and investments, several different methods usually come to mind: savings accounts, certificates of deposit, bonds, etc. But one that may not readily come to mind is investment in U.S. Treasury Bills. U.S. Treasury Bills are among the most marketable securities in the world. They are issued at less than face value and then redeemed at face value on a specified maturity date, within a year or less. However, you have the nice option of being able to sell these bills on the open market before the maturity date. If you do, though, it's a good idea to know the interest rate being earned by the bill so that you won't lose in the transaction.

Consider a hypothetical example: Let's say that a $250 Treasury Bill is sold for $244.33 and it matures in 90 days.
a) Find the annual percent of interest earned.
b) If you have a chance to sell the bill for $247.92 after 60 days, will this be a higher or lower interest rate than you found in part a)?
Solution: The interest, I, is given by
I = PRT where

     I = interest earned in dollars,
     P = principal
     R = annual rate of interest
     T = time in years

We want R, the interest rate, so solving for R gives

$$R = \frac{I}{PT} \text{ (× 100 to get answer in \%)}$$

a) The interest rate $R = \dfrac{(250 - 244.33)}{(244.33)\left(\dfrac{90}{365}\right)} \times 100$

Note: $\left(\dfrac{90 \text{ days}}{365 \text{ days}}\right)$ gives the time in years and I equals money earned or the difference in purchase price and sale price

b) $R = \dfrac{(247.92 - 244.33)}{(244.33)\left(\dfrac{60}{365}\right)} \times 100$

Press	**Display/Comments**

a)

⊂ 250 ⊟ 244.33	
⊃ ÷ ⊂ 244.33 ✕	
⊂ 90 ÷ 365 ⊃ ⊃ ⊟	**0.09411452**
✕ 100 ⊟	**9.4114517** or 9.41%
	interest

b)

⊂ 247.92 ⊟ 244.33	
⊃ ÷ ⊂ 244.33 ✕	
⊂ 60 ÷ 365 ⊃ ⊃ ⊟	**0.08938389**
✕ 100 ⊟	**8.9383893** or 8.94%
	interest

The interest rate for the early sale is lower, so your reasons
for selling the bill would have to outweigh the slight loss!

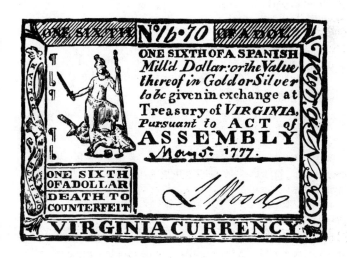

TURNING TO BUSINESS AND FINANCE

Deepening Depreciation

You may have heard the term "depreciation" and wondered about it. Basically, depreciation is a decrease or loss in value because of wear, age, or other cause. This is used more often than not by businesses to help them figure the normal life span of equipment for tax purposes, replacement, etc.

For example: Let's assume a business executive buys new cars for $4200 each which he depreciates at an average rate of 27% of the remaining value per year. This means he will take 27% of the value and subtract it at year's end. This is the same as multiplying the new value by 73%, since 100% − 27% = 73%. Each year the previous year's value is reduced by 27% or multiplied by 73%. Since this particular executive finds it unprofitable to keep cars which are worth less than $1000, how many years should the cars be kept? What is the value of a car after one year, two years, three years, four years, and five years?

Solution:
Let C_0 represent the value of the new car, then 73% of C_0 is the value of the car at the end of the first year (C_1). The value of the car at the end of the second year (C_2) is 73% of the value at the end of the first year or 73% × 73% × C_0, or $C_2 = (73\%)^2 C_0$.

This pattern continues for each year, and in general, C for any year (C_n) is $C_n = (73\%)^n C_0$.

Logarithms can be used, but the calculator provides a much easier way. The calculator's automatic constant can come into play for this one.

Press	Display/Comments
4200 ☒	

.73 ☲	**3066.** value after 1 year
☲	**2238.18** value after 2 years
☲	**1633.8714** value after 3 years
☲	**1192.7261** value after 4 years
☲	**870.69007** value after 5 years

During the 5th year, the car
should be sold.

TURNING TO BUSINESS AND FINANCE
Interest Paid and Earned

A friend of yours poses an interesting question. It seems to your friend that borrowing $1000 *costs* a lot more in interest than you *earn* in interest if you deposit $1000 in a savings account. You know it costs more to borrow — but how much? Assume the finance company's interest rate is 1.01% per month and that the savings account earns 5.5% compounded quarterly.

To solve this problem, you have to make two calculations. The first determines what the finance company will charge for financing the $1000, and the second is to calculate how much money the $1000 earns in a savings account during the same time period. Assume a time period of 36 months.

First, find the interest charge to finance the $1000. Remember, you will be making equal monthly payments for the entire 36 months.

Use this formula:

$$I = nP\left[\frac{1 - (1 + i)^{-n}}{i}\right]^{-1} - P \text{ where}$$

n = number of monthly payments
i = monthly interest
P = principal

This formula is not as difficult as it looks.

Press	Display/Comments
	Note the use of [+/-] to make the exponent 36 into −36. Use of the [−] key to do this results in an error.
1 [−] [(] [(] 1 [+] .0101 [)] [yˣ] 36 [+/-] [)] [=]	**0.30356171** Note: Wait for the number in the display to complete before proceeding.
[÷] .0101 [=] [yˣ] 1 [+/-] [×] 36 [×] 1000 [−] 1000 [=]	**1197.7795** (again, wait) **197.77954** interest charged by finance agent.

Now calculate the interest earned in the savings account using this formula:

$I = P(1 + i)^n - P$ where
i = interest rate per compounding period
n = number of interest compounding periods
P = principal.

Note: Since the interest rate is 5.5% per year compounded quarterly, i will equal $\frac{5.5\%}{4}$. Also, since the loan is for 36 months or 3 years, there will be 12 quarters, so n = 12.

Press	Display/Comments
1 [+] [(] .055 [÷] 4 [)] [=] [yˣ] 12 [×] 1000 [−] 1000 [=]	**1178.0681** **178.06812** interest earned from savings

In borrowing $1000 for 3 years you not only *have* to make monthly payments, but you pay $197.79 interest. If you deposit $1000 in savings, you earn $178.07 interest.

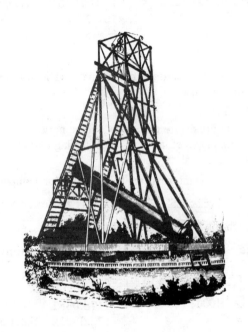

LATCHING ONTO TRIGONOMETRY
Introduction: The Story of Trigonometry

If you look around you carefully, at buildings, desks, chairs, signs, and other structures you encounter, you'll notice that triangles are everywhere. Indeed, the triangle should be thought of as a friendly thing — it adds strength to structures, allows for support for signs, aids in navigation, and has a wide variety of other useful applications. The early Greek mathematicians (sharp as they were) realized that triangles were important — and would continue to be important, so they invented a whole science devoted to studying triangles: TRIGONOMETRY.

A very important part of trigonometry focuses on a special type of triangle that is found especially often in nature, called *right triangles.* Many of you are probably familiar with right triangles, but, for those who aren't, a quick review:

The Story of Right Triangles

First of all, this is an angle ⟨——— . An angle is how we describe the way in which two lines or surfaces touch each other. Angles can be measured in one of three common types of units: degrees, radians, or grads (see *Basic Keys* section), and are usually labelled with Greek letters (like Θ — "theta").
Some angles:

small angle	bigger angle	right angle	bigger angle	straight angle
"acute" angles			"obtuse" angles	

Notice the angle in the center is called a *right angle,* and is an especially common type of angle. (The corner of this book, the floor meeting the wall, etc. — all form right angles.)

Angles smaller than a right angle are called "acute" angles, while angles larger than a right angle are called "obtuse" angles. The most common unit you'll see for measuring angles is the "degree", which is defined as 1/360 of a circle:

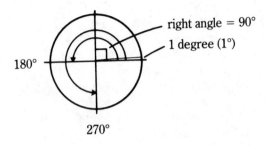

A *right* angle is one that contains ninety degrees (90°). Now, triangles have 3 angles, and in right triangles one of these is a *right* angle.

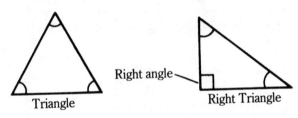

Right triangles pop up all over the place, and the Greeks wanted to be able to describe all of the parts of this type of triangle, and how they are related. To do this, they identified three relationships in right triangles that have stood the test of time and are still popular today!

The "Trig Functions"

These relationships are called the SINE, COSINE, AND TANGENT functions. Here's how they work:

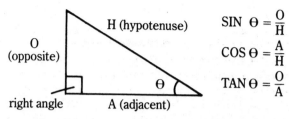

$$\text{SIN } \Theta = \frac{O}{H}$$

$$\text{COS } \Theta = \frac{A}{H}$$

$$\text{TAN } \Theta = \frac{O}{A}$$

In the triangle above — just find Θ, the angle we'll be talking about. The side of the triangle straight across from the angle Θ is called the *opposite* side to Θ, labelled "O". Next, find the right angle, and notice that the side across from it has the long name "hypotenuse" (that's high-pot'-in-noose), and is labelled H. The other side is next to ("adjacent") to Θ, and is labelled A.

Now here's what the Greeks discovered: The lengths of the sides of the triangle were related to the size of the angle Θ as follows:

$$\text{SINE } \Theta = \frac{\text{Length of Opposite Side}}{\text{Length of Hypotenuse}}$$

$$\text{COSINE } \Theta = \frac{\text{Length of Adjacent Side}}{\text{Length of Hypotenuse}}$$

$$\text{TANGENT } \Theta = \frac{\text{Length of Opposite Side}}{\text{Length of Adjacent Side}}$$

These three functions are very important, so three keys on your calculator are devoted entirely to them: $\boxed{\text{sin}}$, $\boxed{\text{cos}}$, $\boxed{\text{tan}}$. (See *Basic Keys* section for additional details.) The rest of this chapter is devoted to examples of how these functions can be useful — at home and in trig class — and how your calculator can make handling trigonometry problems easy, more accurate, and even fun.

There's more on trigonometry, including many handy formulas and identities, in the *Appendix*.

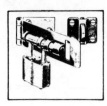

LATCHING ONTO TRIGONOMETRY
Trig on Keys

Four keys on your calculator will be helpful in handling problems involving trigonometry. (See *Basic Keys*
section for more on these keys.)

Your calculator may have a switch or a key that selects
the angular units of measure you want to use in a problem:
Degrees, Radians, or Grads. These 3 units for angle measurement are illustrated below:

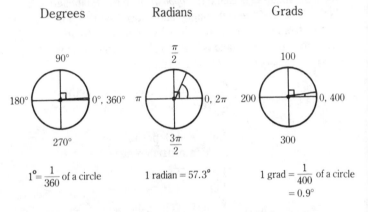

Degrees	Radians	Grads

$1° = \dfrac{1}{360}$ of a circle   1 radian = 57.3° $1 \text{ grad} = \dfrac{1}{400}$ of a circle
= 0.9°

Be sure that the calculator is in the *correct mode* before
performing any calculations involving trig. Your calculator will
assume that any angles you enter are measured in the units
specified by its mode setting. Check your owner's manual for
specifics on how to set degrees, radians and grads on your
calculator.

$\boxed{\text{sin}}$ $\boxed{\text{cos}}$ $\boxed{\text{tan}}$ — These keys assume that the number in the display is an angle, measured in the units you've selected . When you press one of these keys the sin, cos or tan appears in the display. This calculation happens right away — and doesn't affect other calculations in progress.

Many calculators have an inverse or second function key which, when pressed before the $\boxed{\text{sin}}$ $\boxed{\text{cos}}$ or $\boxed{\text{tan}}$ keys, computes the arcsine, arccosine or arctangent of the number in the display. Answers are in degrees, radians or grads, depending on the angular mode you select.

For example, use the $\boxed{\text{2nd}}$ or $\boxed{\text{INV}}$, as follows:

$\boxed{\text{INV}}$ $\boxed{\text{sin}}$ calculates the arcsine ($\sin^{-1}$). This instructs the calculator to find the smallest angle whose sine is in the display. (First or fourth quadrant).

$\boxed{\text{INV}}$ $\boxed{\text{cos}}$ calculates the arccosine ($\cos^{-1}$). This instructs the calculator to find the smallest angle whose cosine is in the display. (First or second quadrant).

$\boxed{\text{INV}}$ $\boxed{\text{tan}}$ calculates the arctangent ($\tan^{-1}$). This instructs the calculator to find the smallest angle whose tangent is in the display. (First or fourth quadrant).

Note: In this book, we will use the key symbol, $\boxed{\text{INV}}$ to show taking the arcsine, arccosine, and arctangent.

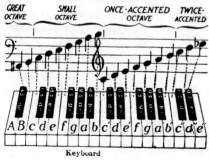

Keyboard

LATCHING ONTO TRIGONOMETRY
Angle Conversions —
Degrees/Radians/Grads

You may sometimes find it necessary to convert angular values from one unit system to another. While your calculator has no special conversion keys for this purpose, the key sequences to convert angular units are pretty easy, and can be used without affecting anything you may have stored in memory, or other calculations in progress. First, be sure the calculator is in the *correct angular mode for entry of the angle to be converted.*

Then,
(1) take the sin of the number (sin)
(2) change to the angular mode you want, and
(3) take the arcsine of the number (INV sin)

Note:
The angular range of the above conversions must be limited to the first and fourth quadrants:
0 ± 90 degrees
$0 \pm \pi/2$ radians
0 ± 100 grads

Here's an example: Express 50 degrees in radians, and then in grads.

Press	Display/Comments
OFF ON/C	This makes certain you are in *degree mode* — all set to enter 50°.
50 sin DRG* INV sin	**.87266463** This is 50 degrees in radians. (*Note:* Be sure to allow enough time for your calculator to finish working when using the trig keys)
sin DRG* INV sin	**55.555556** This is 50 degrees expressed in grads.

*This symbol is used to represent the key or switch on your calculator for changing from degrees to radians to grads.

For converting angles in any quadrant from one system to another, the following table of conversion factors can be used.

FROM	TO degrees	radians	grads
degrees		$\times \dfrac{\pi}{180}$	$\div\ 0.9$
radians	$\times \dfrac{180}{\pi}$		$\times \dfrac{200}{\pi}$
grads	$\times\ 0.9$	$\times \dfrac{\pi}{200}$	

Note that these calculations are performed without using any trig function keys, so they don't depend on the setting of the DRG key. (Be certain your calculator is in correct angular mode if you're using conversion results as part of another trig problem.)

Example: Convert 120 degrees to radians, then grads.

Press | **Display/Comments**

120 ⊠ π ÷ 180 ⊟   **2.0943951**   This is 120° expressed in radians.

⊠ 200 ÷ π ⊟   **133.33333**   This is 120° expressed in grads.

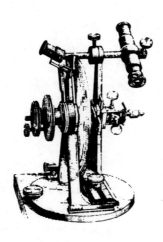

LATCHING ONTO TRIGONOMETRY
Basic "Trig Around the House"

Here are some "around the house" applications of the basic trig functions.

If the sun is at a 30° angle off the horizon at 5 P.M., how far from your 2 meter tall West fence should you start your cactus garden — in order for it to get the full sun until then?

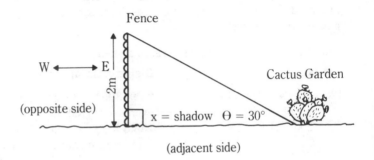

Fence

W ← → E

2m

(opposite side)

x = shadow   Θ = 30°

Cactus Garden

(adjacent side)

Solution: Given one side (2m) and one angle (30°) of a right triangle, you can find the length of any one of its other sides (x). To find x, you can use the formula:

$$\text{Tan } \Theta = \frac{\text{Length of side opposite } \Theta}{\text{Length of side adjacent to } \Theta}$$

$$\tan 30° = \frac{2 \text{ meters}}{x}, \text{ so}$$

$$x = \frac{2}{\tan 30°}$$

(Before you begin, be sure that you are in "degree" mode.)

Press

2 ÷ 30 [tan] [=]

Display/Comments

3.4641016 m — Putting your cactus garden at least this far away will keep it in the sun until 5 P.M.

Here's another one:

You have the happy chore of erecting a TV antenna.
You decide that the guy wires should be at a 35° angle with
respect to your roof, and that you'll need 3 of them.
How much guy wire do you need, if your antenna is 4 meters
high? How far away from the antenna base should you put the
roof supports?

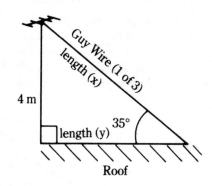

Solution:

$$\text{Sin } 35° = \frac{4 \text{ m}}{\text{length of guy (x)}} \qquad \tan 35° = \frac{4 \text{ m}}{y}$$

$$\text{so, } x = \frac{4 \text{ m}}{\sin 35°} \qquad y = \frac{4 \text{ m}}{\tan 35°}$$

Press	**Display/Comments**
4 ÷ 35 sin =	**6.9737872** Length of one guy wire. (Allow time for your calculator to compute the sine.)
× 3 =	**20.921362** Pick up at least 21 meters of wire.
4 ÷ 35 tan =	**5.7125921** Anchor the wire about 5.7 meters away from the base.

Trig and Land Area

Your calculator and its trig function capability can help you in getting the "lay of the land". *Here's an example:*

You're looking over a piece of property that's bounded by 2 farm roads that intersect at right angles, and a state highway that cuts across at a 20° angle as shown. The previous owner just put a fence around the land, and tells you it took 750 meters of fence. What's the area of the land in square meters (m²)?

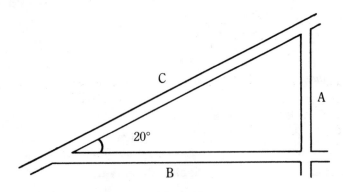

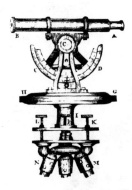

Solution:
The formula for the area of a triangle tells you:
AREA OF LAND = 1/2 A × B

You also know:
A + B + C = 750.

Now

$\tan 20° = \dfrac{A}{B}$, so $B = \dfrac{A}{\tan 20°}$

$\sin 20° = \dfrac{A}{C}$, so $C = \dfrac{A}{\sin 20°}$. Substituting:

$A + \dfrac{A}{\tan 20°} + \dfrac{A}{\sin 20°} = 750.$

$$A\left(1 + \frac{1}{\tan 20°} + \frac{1}{\sin 20°}\right) = 750$$

$$A = \frac{750}{\left(1 + \dfrac{1}{\tan 20°} + \dfrac{1}{\sin 20°}\right)}.$$

Looks tough, you say? At this point your calculator is
ready to take action. Just key in the right side of this
equation carefully — and allow time for your calculator to
"digest" the problem.

Press   Display/Comments

750 ÷ (1 + 20 tan 1/x
+ 20 sin 1/x) = STO   **112.42217** m   This is the
length of side A in meters.
Now to find B:
÷ 20 tan =   **308.87738** m   (length of B)
Next, to find the area
× RCL ÷ 2 =   **17362.333** m² — the land area.

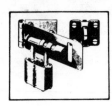

Keys to Quick Graphs

There are some ways to explore mathematics that are made much easier now that you're doing math "on keys". One of these is *graphing*. Drawing a graph of a function shows you how it "works"; and you may be surprised at the symmetry, beauty, and intriguing behavior of trig-related functions. Your calculator can make graphing these functions a cinch!

For example: Graph the function:

$$f(\Theta) = \frac{\tan \Theta}{(1 - \sin \Theta)}$$

for $\Theta = 0°, 30°, 45°, 60°, 90°, 135°, 180°$

Press

		Display/Comments

0 [tan] [÷] [( )] 1 [−] 0 [sin] [ )] [=]   **0.**   (For $\Theta = 0°$, $f(\Theta) = 0$)

30 [tan] [÷] [( )] 1 [−] 30 [sin] [ )] [=]   **1.1547005**
For $\Theta = 30°$, $f(\Theta)$ = about 1.2

45 [tan] [÷] [( )] 1 [−] 45 [sin] [ )] [=]   **3.4142136**
For $\Theta = 45°$, $f(\Theta)$ = about 3.4

60 [tan] [÷] [( )] 1 [−] 60 [sin] [ )] [=]   **12.928203**
For $\Theta = 60°$, $f(\Theta)$ = about 12.9

90 [tan] [÷] [( )] 1 [−] 90 [sin] [ )] [=]   **Error**
For $\Theta = 90°$, $f(\Theta)$ is undefined.

135 [tan] [÷] [( )] 1 [−] 135 [sin] [ )] [=] **−3.4142136**
For $\Theta = 135°$, $f(\Theta)$ is about −3.4

180 [tan] [÷] [( )] 1 [−] 180 [sin] [ )] [=] **0.**
For $\Theta = 180°$, $f(\Theta) = 0$.

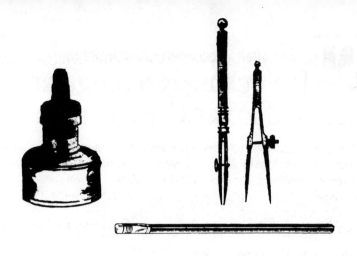

If you graph these points as shown — you begin to see an interesting function "picture". Fill in a few more points! What can you tell about this function from its picture?

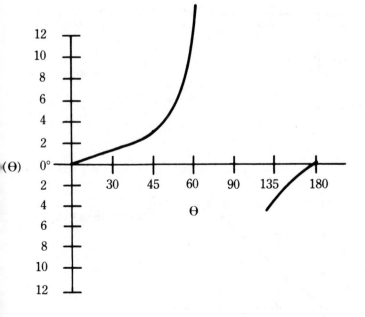

(Θ)

θ

LATCHING ONTO TRIGONOMETRY
Unlocking Rectangular and Polar Coordinates

There are two common ways you can use to locate a point in a plane. You can specify its rectangular coordinates or its polar coordinates.

In the rectangular coordinate system, point (x, y) is located at a distance "x" along the horizontal axis and a distance "y" along the vertical axis. In the polar coordinate system, point (r, Θ) is located at a distance "r" from the origin, and at an angle "Θ" from the horizontal axis (as shown below).

Often you may find that you need to convert between these two representations — and your calculator can simplify this process. The formulas you'll need for these conversions are given below.

rectangular coordinates

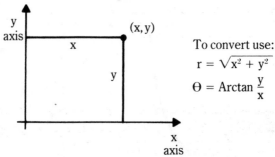

To convert use:
$$r = \sqrt{x^2 + y^2}$$
$$\Theta = \text{Arctan} \frac{y}{x}$$

polar coordinates

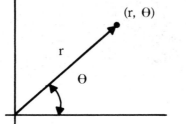

To convert use:
$$x = r \cos \Theta$$
$$y = r \sin \Theta$$

Here's an example: x = 5, y = 6

Transform the rectangular coordinates (5,6) to polar coordinates. Make sure your calculator is in the degree mode.

Press   **Display/Comments**

[OFF] [ON/C]   This makes certain that you
                                               are in degree mode.

5 [x²] [+] 6 [x²] [=] [√x]   **7.8102497** $r = \sqrt{x^2 + y^2}$

6 [÷] 5 [=] [INV] [tan]   **50.194429** $\Theta = \text{ARCTAN} \left(\dfrac{y}{x}\right)$

                                               so r = 7.8, Θ = 50.2°

Convert the polar coordinates (7.8102497, 50.194429) back to rectangular coordinates. Are you in degree mode?

Press   **Display/Comments**

7.8102497 [X] 50.194429 [cos] [=]   **5.**   x = r cos Θ
7.8102497 [X] 50.194429 [sin] [=]   **6.**   y = r sin Θ
                                               Answer: (5,6)
                                                       (x = 5, y = 6)

LATCHING ONTO TRIGONOMETRY
Rectangular and Spherical Coordinates

Many people who apply trig to real life problems need methods of mathematically locating points in 3 dimensional space (navigators, space scientists, air traffic controllers, etc.) There are several methods available, and the problem of converting from one method to another is a common one — and one easily handled with your calculator.

The most common coordinate system is the Rectangular system for specifying a point in space. Three axes (x, y, & z) are used that intersect at one common point called the origin: any point (x, y, z) is located x units along the direction of the x-axis, y units along the direction of the y-axis, and z-units along the z-axis.

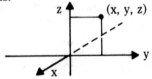

An alternate system that utilizes *angles* to locate the point is the spherical coordinate system. In this system a point

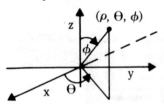

(ρ, Θ, ϕ) is located Θ degrees away from the x-axis in the x-y plane, ϕ degrees from the z-axis, and a distance ρ from the origin.

To transform the *rectangular coordinates* (x, y, z) to spherical coordinates (ρ, Θ, ϕ), use these formulas:

$$\rho = \sqrt{x^2 + y^2 + z^2} \quad \Theta = \text{ARCTAN } \frac{y}{x}, \phi = \text{ARCCOS } \frac{z}{\sqrt{(x^2 + y^2 + z^2)}}$$

To transform *the spherical coordinates (ρ, Θ, ϕ) to rectangular coordinates* (x, y, z), uses these formulas: $x = \rho \sin \phi \cos \Theta$, $y = \rho \sin \phi \sin \Theta$, $z = \rho \cos \phi$

The following examples show how the coordinates are transformed from one system to the next, using the calculator to make the process much easier and more accurate.

Example:

An airplane beginning its landing approach is 2 km east (x),
4 km north (y) and at 5 km altitude (z) with respect to a
control tower. Find the angles a directional radar antenna
should be aimed to spot the plane (Θ, and ϕ), and the distance
the radar signal will have to travel (ρ).

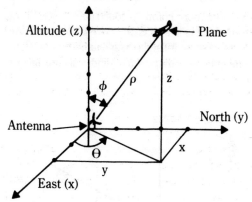

This amounts to converting (x, y, and z) to (ρ, Θ, ϕ).

Press

2 [x²] [+] 4 [x²] [+] 5 [x²] [=]
[√x] [STO]

4 [÷] 2 [=] [INV] [tan]

5 [÷] [RCL] [=] [INV] [cos]

Display/Comments

$\rho = \sqrt{x^2 + y^2 + z^2} =$

6.7082039 kilometers
$\Theta = \text{Arctan } (y/x) =$
63.434949 degrees
$\phi = \text{Arccos } (z/\rho)$
$(z/\sqrt{x^2 + y^2 + z^2}) =$
Arccos (z/ρ)
41.810315 degrees

Here's another example:

Convert the spherical coordinates $\rho = 2.1$, $\Theta = 7°$, $\phi = 46°$
to rectangular coordinates. (First, be sure you're in degree mode.)

Press

2.1 [X] 46 [sin] [X] 7 [cos] [=]

2.1 [X] 46 [sin] [X] 7 [sin] [=]

2.1 [X] 46 [cos] [=]

Display/Comments

x = ρ sin ϕ cos Θ
1.4993537
y = ρ sin ϕ sin Θ
0.18409749
z = ρ cos ϕ
1.4587826
Answer: (1.50, 0.18,
1.46)

Rectangular and Cylindrical Coordinates

We'll cover one more common coordinate system for specifying where something is in space: the *cylindrical coordinate system*. Here are the formulas you'll need for converting from rectangular coordinates to cylindrical coordinates, and vice versa:

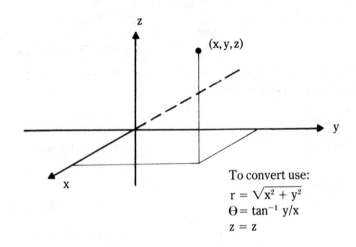

To convert use:

$$r = \sqrt{x^2 + y^2}$$
$$\Theta = \tan^{-1} y/x$$
$$z = z$$

To convert use:

$$x = r \cos \Theta$$
$$y = r \sin \Theta$$
$$z = z$$

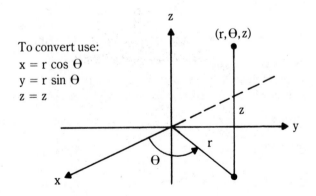

Examples:

Try converting the rectangular coordinates (5, 10, 15) to cylindrical coordinates. Remember to work in degree mode.

Press

5 $\boxed{x^2}$ $\boxed{+}$ 10 $\boxed{x^2}$ $\boxed{=}$ $\boxed{\sqrt{x}}$

10 $\boxed{\div}$ 5 $\boxed{=}$ $\boxed{\text{INV}}$ $\boxed{\tan}$

Display/Comments

$r = \sqrt{x^2 + y^2} =$
11.18034
$\Theta = \tan^{-1} y/x =$
63.434949°
$z = z = 15$
Answer: (11.18, 63.43°, 15)

Now convert the cylindrical coordinates (r = 1, $\Theta = 45°$, z = 1) to rectangular coordinates.

Press

1 $\boxed{\times}$ 45 $\boxed{\cos}$ $\boxed{=}$

1 $\boxed{\times}$ 45 $\boxed{\sin}$ $\boxed{=}$

Display/Comments

$x = r \cos \Theta$
0.70710678
$y = r \sin \Theta$
0.70710678
$z = z = 1$
Answer: (0.71, 0.71, 1)

LATCHING ONTO TRIGONOMETRY
Law of Cosines

Law(s) of Cosines are very helpful in finding sides and angles of any triangle, given two sides and an angle to begin with. Let's take a look at how the Law of Cosines comes about.

Given a triangle with angles a, b, and c and sides opposite, A, B, and C, respectively, draw a perpendicular from c to C and call it "x". Take a look at triangle Bxy, and the following implications:

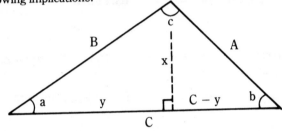

	Reason
1) $B^2 = y^2 + x^2$	Pythagorean theorem
2) $x^2 = B^2 - y^2$	subtraction
3) $A^2 = x^2 + (C-y)^2$	Pythagorean theorem
4) $A^2 = (B^2 - y^2) + (C-y)^2$	substitution
5) $\quad = B^2 - y^2 + C^2 - 2Cy + y^2$	
6) $\quad = B^2 + C^2 - 2Cy$	
7) $\cos a = y/B$	definition of cosine
8) $y = B \cos a$	multiplication
9) $A^2 = B^2 + C^2 - 2BC \cos a$	substitution (8 in 6)

Using similar geometric and algebraic properties, you can derive these *Law(s) of Cosines:*

$$A^2 = B^2 + C^2 - 2BC \cos a$$
$$B^2 = A^2 + C^2 - 2AC \cos b$$
$$C^2 = A^2 + B^2 - 2AB \cos c$$

Problem: Given the same triangle with B = 6.21 meters,
C = 9.62 meters and a = 61°, find A and b.

Formula: $A^2 = B^2 + C^2 - 2BC \cos a$ (Law of Cosines)
First, find A.

Press	Display/Comments
6.21 $\boxed{x^2}$ $\boxed{+}$ 9.62 $\boxed{x^2}$ $\boxed{-}$ $\boxed{(}$ 2 $\boxed{\times}$	$A^2 = 6.21^2 + 9.62^2 -$
	$2(6.21)\,(9.62)\,(\cos 61)$
6.21 $\boxed{\times}$ 9.62 $\boxed{\times}$ 61 $\boxed{\cos}$ $\boxed{)}$	$= 73.183253$ meters^2
$\boxed{=}$ $\boxed{\sqrt{x}}$	**8.5547211** meters = A

Formula: $B^2 = A^2 + C^2 - 2AC \cos b$. Therefore:

$$\cos b = \frac{B^2 - A^2 - C^2}{-2AC}, \text{ so}$$

$$b = \text{Arccos } (B^2 - A^2 - C^2/ -2AC)$$

Press	Display/Comments
6.21 $\boxed{x^2}$ $\boxed{-}$ 8.5547211 $\boxed{x^2}$ $\boxed{-}$	$B^2 - A^2 - C^2 =$
9.62 $\boxed{x^2}$ $\boxed{=}$ $\boxed{STO}$	**−127.16355**
2 $\boxed{\times}$ 8.5547211 $\boxed{\times}$ 9.62 $\boxed{=}$	$(B^2 - A^2 - C^2) / -2AC =$
$\boxed{+/-}$ $\boxed{1/x}$ $\boxed{\times}$ $\boxed{RCL}$ $\boxed{=}$	**0.77259471**
$\boxed{INV}$ $\boxed{\cos}$	**39.412533** = b

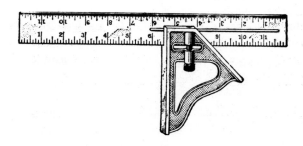

Law of Sines

The *Law of Sines* is another useful relationship for finding the sides and angles of any triangle, given two sides and an angle, or two angles and a side. (As is the *Law of Cosines*, discussed previously.) Given a triangle with angles a, b, and c and sides opposite A, B, and C, respectively, the *Law of Sines* states that:

$$\frac{\sin a}{A} = \frac{\sin b}{B} = \frac{\sin c}{C}$$

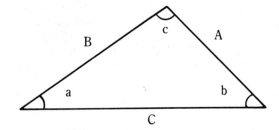

A Quick Example:
In the triangle above, if a = 29°, b = 60° and C = 2 meters, find c, A and B.

To begin, remember that any triangle contains 3 angles that must total up to 180°. So angle c in the triangle can be calculated as follows:

$$c = 180 - a - b$$

Since $\dfrac{\sin a}{A} = \dfrac{\sin c}{C}$, you can rearrange to get

$$A = \frac{C \sin a}{\sin c},$$

Since $\dfrac{\sin a}{A} = \dfrac{\sin b}{B}$, $B = \dfrac{A \sin b}{\sin a}$

on your calculator:

Press

Display/Comments

$C = 180 - a - b =$

180 ⊟ 29 ⊟ 60 ⊜ **91.**

$A = C \sin a / \sin c =$
$(2 \sin 29°) / \sin 91° =$

2 ⊠ 29 sin ⊘ 91 sin ⊜ **0.96976694** meters

$B = A \sin b / \sin a$
$B = .96976694 \sin 60 / \sin 29 =$

⊠ 60 sin ⊘ 29 sin ⊜ **1.7323146** meters

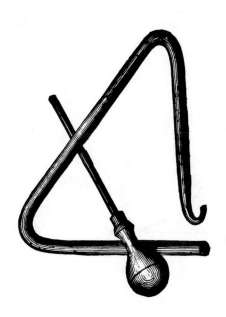

LATCHING ONTO TRIGONOMETRY
Limits of Trig Functions

The behavior of functions is something that you can really explore with your calculator. One aspect of functions that the calculator makes easier to examine is the concept of *limit*. A *limit* is sort of a number that a function can get close to, but never quite arrive at. For example, the limit of the function $\frac{1}{x}$ as x gets closer and closer to zero written $\lim\limits_{x \to 0} \frac{1}{x}$, is infinity. We can write this: $\lim\limits_{x \to 0} \frac{1}{x} = \infty$.

By graphing functions near their limits (with the aid of your calculator), you can spot the trends in the function's behavior and see where it's "headed". This is often a helpful technique for finding the limits of functions that are not obvious.

Consider the following: If we graph $\frac{1}{x}$ for exceedingly small values of x, what happens?

Press		**Display/Comments**
1 ⟨¹⁄ₓ⟩		For x = 1, $\frac{1}{x}$ = **1.**
.5 ⟨¹⁄ₓ⟩		For x = 0.5, $\frac{1}{x}$ = **2.**
.25 ⟨¹⁄ₓ⟩		For x = 0.25, $\frac{1}{x}$ = **4.**
.20 ⟨¹⁄ₓ⟩		For x = 0.20, $\frac{1}{x}$ = **5.**
.125 ⟨¹⁄ₓ⟩		For x = 0.125, $\frac{1}{x}$ = **8.**
.120 ⟨¹⁄ₓ⟩		For x = 0.120, $\frac{1}{x}$ = **8.3333333**

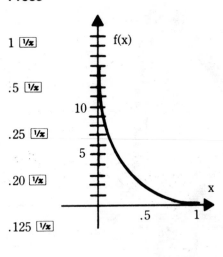

	For $x = 0.100$, $\frac{1}{x} =$
.100 $\boxed{1/x}$	**10.**
	For $x = 0.005$, $\frac{1}{x} =$
.005 $\boxed{1/x}$	**200.**

The smaller x is, the larger $\frac{1}{x}$ is. By observing the trends in this function you could see for yourself that the limit of $\frac{1}{x} = \infty$, as x→0.

Now, some functions have limits that are not obvious at all, and graphing them will let you see the trends in their behavior that will lead you to the limit. *For example:* you now know that $\lim\limits_{x \to 0} \frac{1}{x} = \infty$. You also can look up the fact that as x→0 tan x→0. So think about this: What's the limit as x approaches 0, of the function,
$$f(x) = \frac{\tan x}{x} ?$$

To check this out set your calculator in *radian* mode and examine the trends:

Press

Display/Comments

1 $\boxed{tan}$ $\boxed{\div}$ 1 $\boxed{=}$

$f(1) =$
1.5574077

.5 $\boxed{tan}$ $\boxed{\div}$ .5 $\boxed{=}$

$f(0.5) =$
1.092605

.1 $\boxed{tan}$ $\boxed{\div}$ .1 $\boxed{=}$

$f(0.1) =$
1.0033467

.01 $\boxed{tan}$ $\boxed{\div}$ .01 $\boxed{=}$

$f(0.01) =$
1.0000332

Graphing f(x) for $x = 1, 0.5, 0.1$ and 0.01 can help you see that $\lim\limits_{x \to 0} \frac{\tan x}{x} = 1$.

Try evaluating $\lim\limits_{x \to 0} \sin\left(\frac{1}{x}\right)$ using trends.
What can you tell about this function?

Vectors

What are vectors? Quantities, like forces and velocities, in which the direction as well as the magnitude is important, are called *vectors*.

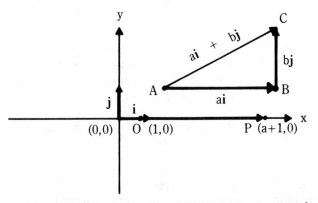

How are they represented? By a directed line segment whose direction represents the direction of the vector and whose length (in terms of some chosen unit of length) represents the magnitude. The unit vector **i** along the x-axis and **j** along the y-axis are vectors whose length is 1. Every vector in the plane may be expressed in terms of **i** and **j**. Two vectors are equal provided they have the *same direction* and the *same magnitude*. So, as can be observed above, vector **AB** is equal to a**i** and vector OP is also equal to a**i**. Therefore **AB = OP**.

OK, here's an example of one application of "vector" math:
You need to cross a stream. The current flows at 15 km/hr.,
and the maximum boat speed (relative to the water) is 25 km/hr.
What angle should you point the boat upstream to arrive directly
opposite on the other side? With what actual speed (relative
to the earth) will you travel?

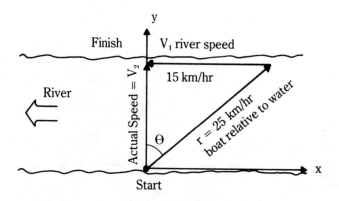

Solution: Let V_1 = the speed at which the river flows and
r = the speed of the boat relative to the water. Find the speed
(V_2) and angle (Θ) of your boat. By examination of the diagram
shown ,

$$V_2 = \sqrt{r^2 - V_1^2} = \sqrt{25^2 - 15^2}$$

$$\sin \Theta = \frac{V_1}{r} = \frac{V_1}{25} \qquad \qquad \Theta = \sin^{-1} \frac{V_1}{25}$$

Press

25 $\boxed{x^2}$ $\boxed{-}$ 15 $\boxed{x^2}$ $\boxed{=}$ $\boxed{\sqrt{x}}$

15 $\boxed{\div}$ 25 $\boxed{=}$ $\boxed{INV}$ $\boxed{sin}$

Display/Comments
actual speed V_2 =
20 km/hr
Θ upstream =
36.869898 degrees

Introduction

In moving through your life, you may encounter a variety of problems or situations where risk or chance is involved. The actual result of the situation hasn't happened yet — but you'd like to know what the chances are that things will work out for the best. What outcome is most probable? What are the chances it will rain on your picnic? What are the odds that you can drive your car coast to coast without a breakdown? What's the chance that your next card will be the ace of spades? Probability won't tell your fortune exactly, but based on a study of the situation the science of probability may give you an idea of what the "odds" are of a certain outcome.

Likewise in some related problem situations you're faced with a large amount of data and need to spot trends, to see the type of event occurring most often, or to "boil down" the facts to a form that's useful. The science of *statistics* can help you here. Working with your calculator to calculate mean values, standard deviations, etc., statistical problems — whether it's batting averages, grades on an exam, mean temperature in an area — whatever — become less hassle with your calculator.

This chapter contains a selection of example situations designed to show you how your calculator can help "crack" the world of probability and statistics. Several special features of your calculator will be especially helpful here.

The science of probability describes many natural phenomena such as the movement of electrons, chemical reactions, the life cycle of stars, etc. You can also see probability in action in a variety of games of chance.

CRACKING PROBABILITY & STATISTICS
Basic Keys
to Probability

Here are a few examples which may open up an idea of your "chances" in various games.

Example 1:
Assume that your name has been placed in a box with 99 other names. What is the probability that your name will be selected for the prize?

The way to predict your chance of winning is to divide the *total number of ways you can win by the total number of possibilities.* In this case, there is only one way for you to win and there are 100 possibilities. Your chance of winning is 1 out of 100 which is $\frac{1}{100}$ or 0.01. In other words, if you entered many, many such contests, you would win about 1 out of 100.

Example 2: If you have shuffled a deck of cards, what is the probability that the top card is the queen of spades?

Since there are 52 cards and only one queen of spades, the probability is 1 ÷ 52.

Press

1 ÷ 52 =

Display/Comments

0.01923077 is the probability.
This rounds to 0.019

If you shuffled the cards 1000 times, the Queen of Spades would be the top card about 19 times. Want to try your luck?

Example 3: If you roll a standard die, what are the chances of rolling a six?

Each time you roll the die there are 6 equally probable ways for the die to land, so your chance of getting a six on a single roll of a single die is just 1 ÷ 6.

Press

1 ÷ 6 =

Display/Comments

0.16666667 or about
17 times out of 100 tries

CRACKING PROBABILITY & STATISTICS
Dice Probability

Many games are based on the rolling of dice. Have you ever wondered about the chance of obtaining a particular value? One way to get a handle on the chances is to construct a table which shows all possible combinations. In this table you represent the results of a toss of 2 dice as a pair of numbers (e.g., 1, 1 for a roll with two ones, etc.).

Possible Values of One Die

Possible Values of Another Die

	1	2	3	4	5	6
1	11	12	13	14	15	16
2	21	22	23	24	25	26
3	31	32	33	34	35	36
4	41	42	43	44	45	46
5	51	52	53	54	55	56
6	61	62	63	64	65	66

The boxes now contain all the combinations possible. For example, the box 46 represents dice values 4 6 .

Next create another table, where you *add* the values on the 2 dice.

2	3	4	5	6	7
3	4	5	6	7	8
4	5	6	7	8	9
5	6	7	8	9	10
6	7	8	9	10	11
7	8	9	10	11	12

The boxes now contain the sum of each possibility.

What is the probability of rolling a 7? All that you do is count the number of sevens in the table and divide by the total number of possibilities. If you look at these tables you see that for any toss of 2 dice there are a total of 36 possibilities. (That's 6×6 — the number of boxes in the table.) There are 6 sevens (all along a diagonal) so the chance of rolling a seven is 6 ÷ 36, or 1 out of 6.

Press

6 ÷ 36 =

Display/Comments

0.16666667 or about 17 out of 100 rolls.

With this process you can make estimates on other numbers.

CRACKING PROBABILITY & STATISTICS
Permutations

Permutations can tell you the number of arrangements that are possible in given situations. For example, suppose you have three squares ☐ ☐ ☐ . How many different ways can you arrange (one to a square) the letters A, B, and C? One way to figure this out is to chart the possibilities:

You may choose any of the **3** letters for the first square

Then you may choose either of the remaining **2** for the second square

Only **1** choice remains for the third square

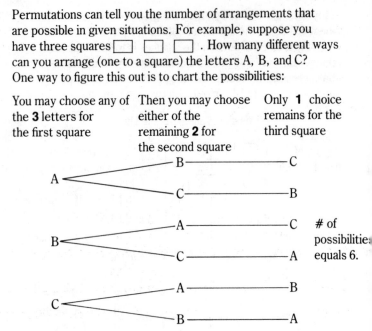

# of possibilities equals 6.

There are six possible arrangements. Three choices for the first square, two choices for the second square, and one choice for the third square. Mathematically, these choices may be thought of as $3 \times 2 \times 1 = 6$. This type of multiplication sequence of 3 is called *3 factorial,* and written as 3 with an exclamation point after it (3!). So: $3! = 3 \times 2 \times 1 = 6$.

Now try this: you have four objects which may be placed in each corner of your room. How many different room arrangements are possible?

There are four choices for the first, three for the second, two for the third and one for the fourth.
$4! = 4 \times 3 \times 2 \times 1 = 24$ possibilities

The number of different arrangements (or permutations) possible in some situations is staggering. Try this: In a class of 17 students with 17 chairs in the classroom, how many different seating charts could a creative teacher produce? That's correct, *17!* (It is easier to multiply factorials "backwards", as illustrated below.)

Press   **Display/Comments**

1 ⨉ 2 ⨉ 3 ⨉ 4 ⨉ 5 ⨉
6 ⨉ 7 ⨉ 8 ⨉ 9 ⨉ 10 ⨉
11 ⨉ 12 ⨉ 13 ⨉ 14 ⨉ 15 ⨉
16 ⨉ 17 =   **3.5569 14** or
                                          355,690,000,000,000

If it took your teacher 10 minutes to make a seating chart, how long would it take to make all the possible seating charts providing, of course, the teacher works 24 hours per day?

$$3.5569 \times 10^{14} \text{ charts} \times \frac{10 \text{ min}}{\text{chart}} \times \frac{1 \text{ hour}}{60 \text{ min}} \times \frac{1 \text{ day}}{24 \text{ h}} \times \frac{1 \text{ year}}{365 \text{ days}} =$$

Press   **Display/Comments**

3.5569 EE↓ 14 ⨉ 10 ÷
60 ÷ 24 ÷ 365 =   **6.7673 09**   That's right!
                                          It would take over 6
                                          billion years.

As you can see, the number of permutations or arrangements can be very numerous even in simple situations. Maybe that's why the world seems to be constantly changing!

A Permutation Taken 3 at a Time

Here's another permutation situation with a new twist. What if you had three squares ☐ ☐ ☐ and were asked how many different arrangements you could make using all the letters of the alphabet (one letter to a square). Could you figure it out?

How many possibilities would you have to fill the first square? *26*. That would leave *25* for the second square and *24* possibilities for the third. The total number of possibilities is 26 x 25 x 24.

Press   **Display/Comments**

26 ☒ 25 ☒ 24 ☐   **15600.** arrangements

Actually, this is a sort of upper limit (15,600) to the total possible number of 3 letter "words" in the English language. In your lifetime you'll probably get to know all of the 2 letter words in the language. Perhaps a more interesting question is: how many *4 letter words* are possible?

General Keys into Permutations

If you were calculating permutations every day, or taking a statistics course or trying to impress your friends, it would be nice to have a formula for the proper procedure.

Consider these special cases: when you arrange three different letters in three squares (one letter to a square) in all possible permutations, the number of permutations is 3! This is often restated by those into "stat" as "the number of permutations of three objects taken three at a time". A shorthand for writing this is $_3P_3$, and would be written $_nP_n$ for any number of objects (n) taken n at a time. $_nP_n = n!$ Now, if you were to arrange all 26 letters of the alphabet in three squares (one to a square), the total number of permutations would be $26 \times 25 \times 24$ (see previous section). This can be restated as the number of permutations of 26 objects taken three at a time. The shorthand for this is

$$_{26}P_3 = 26 \times 25 \times 24.$$

The next step may seem unnecessary, but it will pay off in the long run. $26 \times 25 \times 24$ may be written as $\dfrac{26!}{(26 - 3)!}$. Notice that the $(26 - 3)!$ in the denominator just "cancels" off all of 26! except the desired 26 x 25 x 24. Now the example may be written as $_{26}P_3 = \dfrac{26!}{(26 - 3)!}$. This allows you to get to a general formula for the permutations of n objects taken r at a time (r would be 3 in this example)!

$$_nP_r = \frac{n!}{(n - r)!}.$$

This formula applies in general to permutations of distinct objects. You'll probably see it around, and, remember, it's not hard to understand with your calculator helping you with the mathematics.

Combinations — A Helpful Formula

Sometimes you will not be concerned with the way in which objects are ordered, but only with the *makeup* of the group. For example, suppose you like 10 particular foods, and each day you have someone pack *three* of these in your lunch sack. You don't care with what order they are put in the sack; you just want them to be in there. You might ask yourself how many different *combinations* of foods (different menus) might appear for your lunch?

Calculating this one is not an easy task. Think about it!

The best method of attacking this situation is to come in the "back door", so to speak. First ask yourself how many permutations are possible for the 10 foods, taken three at a time:

$$_{10}P_3 = \frac{10!}{(10-3)!} = 10 \times 9 \times 8$$

Press

10 ✕ 9 ✕ 8 =

Display/Comments

720.

Now notice this: 720 is *not* the number of *combinations* of foods, but the number of *permutations*. In counting permutations a group of foods such as

apple	⎡ is counted separately, along ⎤	cookie
cookie	⎨ with groups that have the ⎬	cheese sandwich
cheese sandwich	⎩ same foods but in a different ⎭	apple
	order, such as:	

In fact *each* of these groups of 3 identical foods was counted 3! or 6 times in the permutation calculation. *That's the key to the difference between permutations and combinations!* The number of combinations in this case:

720 ÷ 6 = **120.**

The number of combinations equals the total number of permutations (720) divided by the number of permutations of each three foods (3!).

The special notation for the number of *combinations* of 10 foods taken three at a time is $\binom{10}{3}$. The general formula for n combinations taken r at a time is

$$\binom{n}{r} = \frac{_nP_r}{r!} = \frac{n!}{r!\,(n-r)!}$$

CRACKING PROBABILITY & STATISTICS
Cards on Keys

Here's an example you may have thought about: How many different poker hands (5 cards) could you be dealt from a deck of 52 cards? Stating this problem mathematically you'd say: what is the number of combinations of 52 things taken 5 at a time? You can use the formula (see previous section):

$$\binom{n}{r} = \frac{n!}{r!\,(n-r)!}$$

$$\binom{52}{5} = \frac{52!}{5!\,(52-5)!} \quad \text{or} \quad \frac{52!}{5!\,(47!)}$$

If you look carefully, you can see that:
$$52! = 52 \times 51 \times 50 \times 49 \times 48 \times 47!$$
So you can cancel 47! from the numerator and denominator of the equation above to get:

$$\binom{52}{5} = \frac{52 \times 51 \times 50 \times 49 \times 48}{5!}$$

$$\binom{52}{5} = \frac{(52 \times 51 \times 50 \times 49 \times 48)}{(5 \times 4 \times 3 \times 2 \times 1)}$$

Press	Display/Comments
$\boxed{(}$ 52 $\boxed{\times}$ 51 $\boxed{\times}$ 50 $\boxed{\times}$ 49 $\boxed{\times}$ 48 $\boxed{)}$ $\boxed{\div}$ $\boxed{(}$ 5 $\boxed{\times}$ 4 $\boxed{\times}$ 3 $\boxed{\times}$ 2 $\boxed{\times}$ 1 $\boxed{)}$ $\boxed{=}$	**2598960.** is the number of possible hands.

What is the probability that you will be dealt a royal flush? Only 4 of the 2,598,960 hands are royal flushes. Your chances are:

Press	Display/Comments
4 $\boxed{\div}$ 2598960 $\boxed{=}$	**0.00000154** are your chances, take $\boxed{1/x}$.
$\boxed{1/x}$	**649740.** You may expect to be dealt a royal flush once out of every 649,740 hands.

The Same Birthday

Probability is full of surprises. Sometimes events which seems very unlikely to our "common sense" are really not so unlikely at all. Assume that you are in a room with 25 people. What are the chances that two of you have the same birthday?

As is sometimes the case in the study of probability this situation is best explored in reverse. So first consider how you would calculate the probability that *no* two people in the room have the same birthday? You then *subtract that probability* from 1, to get the probability of the reverse outcome.

Start with one person. Whatever the day, he or she has a birthday. The probability that another person does not have that day as a birthday is $\frac{364}{365}$. (Assume 365 days in a year.) The probability that a third person does not have the same birthday as the previous two is $\frac{363}{365}$. The pattern continues for each of the 25 people. The probability that all of the people have different birthdays is *the product of all the independent probabilities,* so the probability that no two people have the same birthday is $\frac{364}{365} \times \frac{363}{365} \times$

$\frac{362}{365} \times \frac{361}{365} \times \frac{360}{365} \times \frac{359}{365} \times \frac{358}{365} \times \frac{357}{365} \times \frac{356}{365} \times \frac{355}{365} \times \frac{354}{365} \times$

$\frac{353}{365} \times \frac{352}{365} \times \frac{351}{365} \times \frac{350}{365} \times \frac{349}{365} \times \frac{348}{365} \times \frac{347}{365} \times \frac{346}{365} \times \frac{345}{365} \times$

$\frac{344}{365} \times \frac{343}{365} \times \frac{342}{365} \times \frac{341}{365}$

This calculation would take a long time (it would take some of us forever) without using your calculator. Note that the denominator is 365 to the 24th power. Multiply the numerators first (it is easier to multiply in reverse).

Press	Display/Comments

341 ⊠ 342 ⊠ 343 ⊠ 344 ⊠
345 ⊠ 346 ⊠ 347 ⊠ 348 ⊠
349 ⊠ 350 ⊠ 351 ⊠ 352 ⊠
353 ⊠ 354 ⊠ 355 ⊠ 356 ⊠
357 ⊠ 358 ⊠ 359 ⊠ 360 ⊠
361 ⊠ 362 ⊠ 363 ⊠ 364 ⊟   **1.3484   61**
⊡ ⊏ 365 y^x 24 ⊐ ⊟   **0.4313003** probability of no
two people having the same
birthday.

+/− ⊞ 1 ⊟   **0.5686997**

There is almost a 60% chance of at least two birthdays on
the same day!

Try this: There are 5 people in your office. What's the
probability that 2 of you have the same birthday? (**Ans.:**
Less than 3%)

CRACKING PROBABILITY & STATISTICS
Factorial!

By now you've seen that you often need to compute factorials (n!) when considering problems in probability. (Some calculators have special keys dedicated to this function.) One method of getting to an approximate value of n! that may save some time for large values of n is to use the following formula:

n! is approximately equal to: $\sqrt{2\pi n} \; n^n \; e^{-n}$

The keystroke sequence for this is:

n! = n [X] 2 [X] [π] [=] [√x] [X] n [yˣ] n [X] n
[+/−] [INV] [lnx] [=]

This value will be a close approximation to n!, and will save keystrokes if n is over 8.

Example: calculate 8! — using both "longhand" and the formula approach:

Press

8 [X] 7 [X] 6 [X] 5 [X] 4 [X]
3 [X] 2 [X] 1 [=]
8 [X] 2 [X] [π] [=] [√x] [X]
[(] 8 [yˣ] 8 [)] [X] 8 [+/−] [INV] [lnx]
[=]

Display/Comments

40320.   8! calculated direc[t]

39902.395   8! by formula.

(*Note:* The quantity 0! is defined to be 1.)

CRACKING PROBABILITY & STATISTICS
Average and Median

Possibly the most commonly used statistical calculation is the *average,* and they're easy to handle using your calculator. The word "average" is usually used to refer to a value obtained by adding together a set of measurements and then dividing by the number of measurements in the set. Actually, this is a special type of average and is technically called the *arithmetic mean.*

Example 1: Five racers ran the hundred meter dash. Their times were recorded as 10.4 seconds, 11.5 seconds, 9.9 seconds, 10.5 seconds and 12 seconds. What was the average time for the racers?

Press

10.4 ⌞+⌟ 11.5 ⌞+⌟ 9.9 ⌞+⌟ 10.5
⌞+⌟ 12 ⌞=⌟ ⌞÷⌟ 5 ⌞=⌟

Display/Comments

10.86 seconds is the average time.

The *median* is a value such that half the observations fall above it and half below it.

Example 2: What is the median time in the 100 meter race if the times are 10.4 seconds, 11.5 seconds, 9.9 seconds, 10.5 seconds and 12 seconds? It is easy to spot the median if the times are arranged in order by value. Starting from the shortest time the values are:

> 9.9 seconds
> 10.4 seconds
> 10.5 seconds
> 11.5 seconds
> 12.0 seconds

The median is the middle time (10.5 seconds).
(If the number of data values is an even number, then the average of the *two* middle values is the median.)

A Standard Deviation Story

Once there was a football coach who divided his physical education class into groups of five students and, unfair as it may seem, gave everyone in each group the same grade. The grades were based on the average performance of *each* group. Here's how two groups of five students compared in the activity called "pull up". In group one, Fred and John both did 7 pull ups, and the other members of the group did 5, 6 and 8. In group two, *Joe Stat did 16* and the others did 1, 10, 2 and 4. When grade time rolled around, the coach had his student teacher average the grades.

Press

7 ＋ 7 ＋ 5 ＋ 6 ＋ 8 ＝
＋ 5 ＝

16 ＋ 10 ＋ 2 ＋ 1 ＋ 4 ＝
＋ 5 ＝

Display/Comments

6.6 was the average for Group 1

6.6 was the average for Group 2

As you can see, both groups (everyone) got the same grade. And guess who was mad? You guessed it—Joe Stat. Joe complained about this to the coach, but the grades were already turned in and there was nothing which could be done. The coach said that he would have done something about it, if he had only known, but all he saw were group averages and he wasn't about to look at all the individual scores. Joe resolved to find some way to alert the coach to such large variations in a group's performance, so other stars (such as himself), would not be slighted in the future. Later on, Joe took a statistics class and found what he was looking for—a *measure of how much variation is hidden in averages*. It's called the *standard deviation*.

$$\text{S.D.} = \sqrt{\frac{\sum\limits_{1}^{N} (x - \bar{x})^2}{N - 1}}$$

Where $\overset{N}{\underset{1}{\Sigma}}-$ is a symbol which means the sum from 1 to N.

x represents each score
x̄ represents the average score
N is the number of scores

Joe got out his calculator, and found the standard deviation
for the two groups of scores. (Remember it was previously
calculated that the average score for each group x̄, was 6.6.)
The scores, Group 1: 7, 7, 5, 6, 8
            Group 2: 16, 10, 2, 1, 4

The ⎡K⎤ * key on your calculator, along with the ⎡SUM⎤ or ⎡M+⎤
will really help in this case:

Press   **Display/Comments**

6.6 ⎡−⎤ ⎡K⎤   **6.6** is set up as a constant
                                       for subtraction
7 ⎡=⎤ ⎡x^2⎤ ⎡STO⎤   **0.16**
7 ⎡=⎤ ⎡x^2⎤ ⎡SUM⎤   **0.16**
5 ⎡=⎤ ⎡x^2⎤ ⎡SUM⎤   **2.56**
6 ⎡=⎤ ⎡x^2⎤ ⎡SUM⎤   **0.36**
8 ⎡=⎤ ⎡x^2⎤ ⎡SUM⎤   **1.96**
⎡RCL⎤ ⎡÷⎤ 4 ⎡=⎤ ⎡$\sqrt{x}$⎤   **1.1401754**

6.6 ⎡−⎤ ⎡K⎤
16 ⎡=⎤ ⎡x^2⎤ ⎡STO⎤   **88.36**
10 ⎡=⎤ ⎡x^2⎤ ⎡SUM⎤   **11.56**
2 ⎡=⎤ ⎡x^2⎤ ⎡SUM⎤   **21.16**
1 ⎡=⎤ ⎡x^2⎤ ⎡SUM⎤   **31.36**
4 ⎡=⎤ ⎡x^2⎤ ⎡SUM⎤   **6.76**
⎡RCL⎤ ⎡÷⎤ 4 ⎡=⎤ ⎡$\sqrt{x}$⎤   **6.3087241**

Thus the difference in standard deviation shows that although
the average for each group was the same (6.6), the *individual
folks* in group 2 differed from this average (above or below
it) more than in group one. This measure would be enough
to warn the coach!
Note: Be sure to check your owner's manual for the operation
of the automatic constant on your calculator.

SECURING PHYSICS AND CHEMISTRY
Introduction

Your calculator can be a tool that helps "secure" your explorations in your science classes, or as you find science applied around the home in everyday life. Scientists often work with mathematical "models" of phenomena — numerical descriptions of how the world is put together. Your calculator, equipped with scientific notation, is a "natural" for helping you in quickly and accurately handling scientific math. In this way, your mind may be a little freer — to focus on the whys and hows of physical laws or natural events.

The formulas you'll find in the following sections are usually lettered in a common sense way and related to a diagram or description of the problem. This chapter is a selection of basic problems from physics and chemistry, along with some "astronomical" calculations. These examples are selected to familiarize you with how your calculator can be a great vehicle for exploration in the "basics" of science. You take it from there!

Scientific Notation and the Speed of Light

Your calculator is equipped to handle both the very large and the very small numbers that come up in physics and astronomy. It allows you to manipulate them with relative ease and accuracy, so you can keep your eye on what's going on in the problem.

For example: Light travels incredibly fast!
Speed of light 2.9979×10^8 meters per second
$= 186,000$ miles per second

At the same time, the universe is incredibly large — so large that the light-year (distance light travels in 1 year) is often used as a unit in describing it. So calculate this: if our nearest neighboring star is 4.3 light-years away, how many meters is that? How many years would it take to drive there at 88.5 km/hr (55 mph)?

$$4.3 \text{ light-years} \times \frac{365.24 \text{ days}}{\text{years}} \times \frac{24 \text{ hours}}{\text{day}} \times \frac{3600 \text{ seconds}}{\text{hour}}$$
$$\times \frac{2.9979 \times 10^8 \text{ meters}}{\text{second}} =$$

Press   **Display/Comments**

4.3 ☒ 365.24 ☒ 24 ☒ 3600
  ☒ 2.9979 EE↓ 8 ☐= STO   **4.068   16**   meters to the
                                                      nearest star: 4.068×10^{16}.

To determine the number of years required to drive there at 88.5 kilometers per hour, you might convert 88.5 km/hr to meters per year and divide the total distance by the rate.

$$\frac{88.5 \text{ kilometers}}{\text{hour}} \times \frac{24 \text{ hours}}{\text{day}} \times \frac{365.24 \text{ days}}{\text{year}} \times \frac{1000 \text{ meters}}{\text{kilometer}}$$

Press   **Display/Comments**

88.5 ☒ 24 ☒ 365.24 ☒

1000 ☐=   **7.7577   08** $\frac{\text{meters}}{\text{year}}$

1/x ☒ RCL ☐=   **5.2438   07**   years
                                             A long drive!

Here's another: At 28 miles per gallon, how much gas would it take? You're on your own.

SECURING PHYSICS AND CHEMISTRY
Free Fall

It took until the 17th century for mankind to realize that the acceleration of objects in free fall was a constant (this was one of Galileo's many accomplishments). The acceleration due to gravity is usually labelled with the letter g, and is equal to:

$$g = 9.81 \; \frac{m}{s^2} \quad \text{(metric)} \qquad g = 32.2 \; \frac{ft}{s^2} \quad \text{(English)}$$

An Example:
A rock is thrown into a well 214 meters deep (d) at an initial velocity of 4 m/s (V_o). How long (t) will it take the rock to hit the bottom of the well? (This assumes no "wind resistance" is present).

Formula:

$$d = \frac{1}{2}gt^2 + V_o t,$$

so $\frac{1}{2}gt^2 + V_o t - d = 0$. With our values inserted:

$$\frac{1}{2}(9.81)t^2 + 4t - 214 = 0.$$

$$4.905t^2 + 4t - 214 = 0$$

Use the quadratic formula to solve:

$$t = \frac{-b \pm \sqrt{b^2 - 4ac}}{2a}$$

where a = 4.905
b = 4
c = −214

Press | **Display/Comments**

4 +/− + (4 x² −
(4 × 4.905 × 214 +/−))   Store the radical term.
√x STO   **64.920567**
= ÷ (2 × 4.905) =   **6.2100476**   1st root
(4 +/− − RCL) ÷
(2 × 4.905) =   **−7.025542**   2nd root

Time in this case cannot be negative, so take the positive root. The answer is approximately 6.2 seconds.

SECURING PHYSICS AND CHEMISTRY
Constant
Acceleration Problems:

A whole series of problems in basic physics (that are applicable in a variety of everyday life situations) are solvable with the formulas for motion with constant acceleration — which are discussed in the example below:

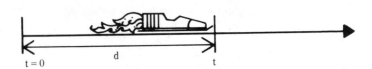

$t = 0$ d   t

For example:
A rocket sled under a constant acceleration (a) raced 300 meters (d) in 5 seconds (t) starting from rest. Find: a) the acceleration; b) the average speed ($\overline{V}$); c) the speed at the end of the 5 seconds (V) and d) the distance traveled in $2\frac{1}{2}$ seconds (d_s).

Formulas: a) $d = \frac{1}{2}at^2$ so $a = \frac{2d}{t^2}$ b) $\overline{V} = \frac{d}{t}$

           c) $V = at$ d) $d_s = \frac{1}{2}at_s^2$

Equations: a) $a = \frac{2\,(300)}{5^2}$ b) $\overline{V} = \frac{300}{5}$

           c) $V = a(5)$ d) $d_s = \frac{1}{2}\,a(2.5)^2$

Press	**Display/Comments**
2 ☒ 300 ÷ 5 $\boxed{x^2}$ = STO	**24.** m/s² = a
300 ÷ 5 =	**60.** m/s = V, (avg. speed)
RCL ☒ 5 =	**120.** m/s = V (velocity at
2 $\boxed{1/x}$ ☒ RCL ☒ 2.5 $\boxed{x^2}$	5 seconds)
=	**75.** m = d_s

Now try this: A car accelerates from rest to 120 m/sec in 7.2 sec. Using $a = V/t$, find the average acceleration. Find the total distance traveled in 7.2 sec. Ans.:

     $a = 16.67$ m/s² $d = 432$ m.

SECURING PHYSICS AND CHEMISTRY
Work — Power

Power is the time rate of doing work; and is commonly measured in watts (or kilowatts). P (watts) $= \dfrac{\text{work (joules)}}{\text{time (seconds)}}$.

Work is calculated as Force × distance:
(If all forces and motions are along the same line.) Here's a problem illustrating how your calculator with scientific notation can help simplify work and power problems:

A large elevator uses a diesel engine with lift power P of 500 kw to pull a cable lift which has a 1000 newton pull F_{DRAG} when empty. The total vertical lift distance (d) is 400 meters. How many 60 kg boxes can the elevator accommodate at one time if the vertical speed (v) of the elevator is 2 m/s?

Solution: First, the total time for the elevator to lift 400 meters can be found from: $t = \dfrac{400 \text{ meters}}{2 \text{ m/s}} = 200$ seconds.

Next, calculate the total work output of the elevator during that time using: W = P × t. Then, use the formula
F_T × distance = work, to calculate the number of boxes:
$F_T = [(\text{\# of boxes}) \times 60 \times 9.8 + F_{drag}]$, so:
$[(\text{\# of boxes}) \times 60 \times 9.8 + F_{drag}] \times d = W$.
Solving: (# of boxes) $= \dfrac{W - F_{drag}\, d}{60 \times 9.8 \times d}$
W = P × t where P = 500kw, t = 200s and
$F_{drag} = 1000$, d = 400 m.

Press

(500,000 ☒ 200)

─ (1000 ☒ 400)
÷ (60 ☒ 9.8 ☒ 400)
═

Display/Comments

1.   08   This is W, the total work done by the elevator in 200 s (1×10^8 joules).

423.46939 or 423 boxes.

Keys to Vectors and Force

Forces are vectors which may be resolved into "components" along rectangular axes, using trigonometry as shown below. Your calculator, with its trig function capability, will keep tabs on the mathematics for you:

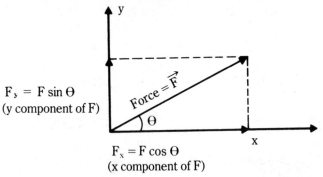

$F_y = F \sin \Theta$
(y component of F)

$F_x = F \cos \Theta$
(x component of F)

Here's an example:
A water skier is pulled simultaneously by two boats running parallel to each other. The boats pull with an equal rope force (F) of 800 N. Each tow rope is 20 m long, and the boats are 5 m apart. With what force (F_t) is the skier actually pulled?

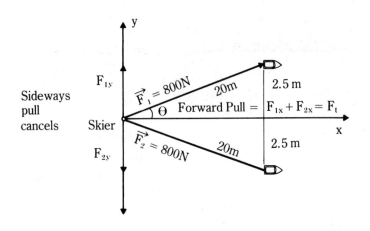

Solution:

Examining the diagram carefully, you can see that the "sideways pull" the boats exert on the skier cancels to zero (since they are equal and opposite in direction), while the forward pull exerted on the skier (F_t) is equal to the sum of the x components of the force exerted by each boat ($F_{1x} + F_{2x}$). Since the force exerted by each boat is the same (800N), the total force can be calculated as just 2 times F_{1x}.

From the diagram:

$$\sin \Theta = \frac{2.5m}{20m}, \; \Theta = \sin^{-1}\left(\frac{2.5}{20}\right)$$

$$\cos \Theta = \frac{F_{1x}}{F}, \; F_{1x} = F \cos \Theta$$

$$F_t = 2F_{1x}$$

On your calculator just calculate Θ, then F_{1x}, then F_t as follows:

Press

2.5 ÷ 20 = INV sin STO
800 X RCL cos =

X 2 =

Display/Comments

7.1807558° = Θ
793.7254 = F_{1x}
(This is the forward force exerted on the skier by 1 boat)

1587.4508 N   The total forward force on the skier, F_t.

Circular Motion

For any object to move in a circle, a force called the *centripetal force* must be applied to it:

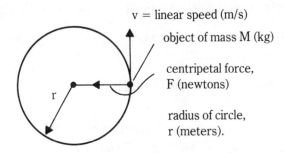

v = linear speed (m/s)

object of mass M (kg)

centripetal force,
F (newtons)

radius of circle,
r (meters).

The centripetal force can be found using the formula:

$$F \text{ (newtons)} = \frac{M \text{ (kg) } v^2 \text{ (m/s)}^2}{r \text{ (m)}}.$$ The centripetal acceleration
is given by $a = \frac{v^2}{r} \text{(m/sec}^2)$.

Example:
You're driving a 1000 kg car and go into a circular turn of radius 60 meters at 60 km/h. What force must your tires and the road provide to keep you in that turn?

$$F = \frac{mv^2}{r} \text{ where m} = 1000 \text{ kg}$$

$$v\left(\frac{m}{sec}\right) = 60 \ \frac{km}{h} \times \frac{h}{3600s} \times \frac{1000m}{km};$$

$$r = 60m$$

Press   **Display/Comments**

1000 $\boxed{\times}$ $\boxed{(}$ 60 $\boxed{\div}$ 3600
$\boxed{\times}$ 1000 $\boxed{)}$ $\boxed{x^2}$ $\boxed{\div}$ 60
$\boxed{=}$ **4629.6296** newtons

That's a little over 1000 lbs — think you'll stay in the turn — or will you "spin out"?

Here's another one:

A model airplane flyer flies a 1.23 kg plane in a circular path at the end of a 15 meter long wire. He needs to calculate the top linear speed (v in m/s) of his plane. With a spring balance scale on the wire, he can tell that at top speed the force on the wire is 50 newtons.

Solution:

Since $F = \dfrac{mv^2}{r}$; $v = \sqrt{\dfrac{rF}{m}}$

where   r = 15 meters
        F = 50 newtons
       m = 1.23 kg

Press   **Display/Comments**

15 $\boxed{\times}$ 50 $\boxed{\div}$ 1.23
$\boxed{=}$ $\boxed{\sqrt{x}}$ **24.69324** m/sec — the plane's top speed. (What's that in mph?)

Simple Lenses

The relationships between images, objects, and distances when you're working with simple lenses are particularly easy to work with on your calculator. (The $\boxed{1/x}$ key is especially helpful here.)

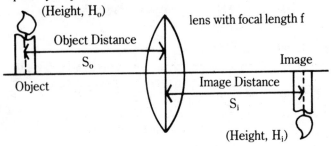

(Height, H_o)

lens with focal length f

Object Distance

S_o

Image

Object

Image Distance

S_i

(Height, H_i)

The two equations that describe this lens situation are:

$$\frac{1}{S_o} + \frac{1}{S_i} = \frac{1}{f}$$

and $\quad \dfrac{H_i}{H_o} = \dfrac{S_i}{S_o}$

Example:
Find the distance from the lens to a *focused image* (S_i) and the *image height* (H_i), if the *object* is 25 cm from the lens (S_o), the lens focal length (f) is 12 cm, and the object is 3 cm tall (H_o).

Solution:
First, rearrange your first equation

$$\frac{1}{S_i} = \frac{1}{f} - \frac{1}{S_o}$$

and solve for S_i, then use $\quad H_i = \dfrac{S_i}{S_o} H_o \quad$ to find H_i.

Press	**Display/Comments**
12 $\boxed{1/x}$ $\boxed{-}$ 25 $\boxed{1/x}$ $\boxed{=}$ $\boxed{1/x}$	**23.076923** cm is the image distance (S_i). Next to find H_i:
$\boxed{\div}$ 25 $\boxed{\times}$ 3 $\boxed{=}$	**2.7692308** cm

SECURING PHYSICS AND CHEMISTRY
Energy and E = mc²

Albert Einstein first wrote the equation above, which is a fundamental relationship between mass and energy. There is a lot of energy "stored" in matter!

(Energy in joules) = (mass in kg) × (speed of light in m/s)².
The speed of light (c) is approximately 2.9979×10^8 m/s.

In addition to the *joule,* another unit scientists use to specify energy is the *electron volt (ev):*

1 electron volt = 1.6022×10^{-19} joules.
energy in joules ÷ 1.6022×10^{-19} = electron volts.

Here are some examples that explore the kinds of numbers involved when discussing mass and energy:
a) Find the Energy equivalent in Mev (Million electron volts) of 1 atomic mass unit (amu = 1.6605×10^{-27} kg).
b) If 1 kg of matter is converted completely to energy, what would the resultant energy be in joules? If 1 joule equals 2.78×10^{-7} kilowatt hours, how many kilowatt hours would be produced? How long would that keep ten 100-watt light bulbs burning? Ten 100 watt bulbs are a 1 kilowatt "load".

Solutions:

Press	Display/Comments		
a)			
1.6605 [EE↓] 27 [+/−] [×]			
2.9979 [EE↓] 8 [x²] [=]	**1.4924**	**−10**	joules per amu: 1.4924×10^{-10}
[÷] 1.6022 [EE↓] 19 [+/−] [=]	**9.3144**	**08**	ev per amu: 9.3144×10^8
[÷] 1 [EE↓] 6 [=]	**9.3144**	**02**	Mev per amu: 931.44
b)			
1 [×] 2.9979 [EE↓] 8 [x²] [=]	**8.9874**	**16**	joules in 1 kg: 8.9874×10^{16}
[×] 2.78 [EE↓] 7 [+/−] [=]	**2.4985**	**10**	kwh in 1 kg: 2.4985×10^{10}

This means if 1 kg of mass could be converted entirely to energy, it would keep ten 100-watt bulbs lit for 2.4985×10^{10} hours, or about 2.9 million years!

What would happen if a *ton* of coal could be *completely converted* to energy?!

SECURING PHYSICS AND CHEMISTRY
Half-Life

Radioactive elements "decay" according to an *exponential* law. If you start out with a sample of radioactive material with some number of atoms (N_o), the number of radioactive atoms left after a time t (N_t) is given by formula

$N_t = N_o \ e^{-kt}$, where k is called the *disintegration constant*. Since your calculator can handle calculations involving logarithms and "e", it will be helpful in handling problems involving radioactivity.

The *half-life* (T) of a radioactive substance is the time it takes for half the sample to decay. If you put $N_t = N_o/2$ and t = T in the equation above, and solve for T you get:

$\dfrac{N_o}{2} = N_o e^{-kT}$ so $\dfrac{1}{2} = e^{-kT}$ Now take $\boxed{\text{ln}x}$ of both sides:

$\ln\left(\dfrac{1}{2}\right) = -kT$

Using your calculator you can quickly compute

$\ln\left(\dfrac{1}{2}\right) = -.69314718$

(Press 1 $\boxed{\div}$ 2 $\boxed{=}$ $\boxed{\text{ln}x}$)

So $-.693 = -kT$, or $T = \dfrac{.693}{k}$

$$\text{Half-life (T)} = \dfrac{0.693}{\text{disintegration constant}}$$

Here's an example:
The disintegration constant of Radium is $k = 1.36 \times 10^{-11} \ s^{-1}$.   a) Find its half-life.
b) If you have a sample of radium containing (N_o) atoms, what fraction of them will be left after 2 years?
Solution:

a) $T = \dfrac{0.693}{1.36 \times 10^{-11}}$ or more precisely $\dfrac{-\ln\left(\dfrac{1}{2}\right)}{1.36 \times 10^{-11}}$

b) $N_t = N_o e^{-kt}$ or $\dfrac{N_t}{N_o} = e^{-1.36 \times 10^{-11}t}$, substitute

    2 years for t (*in seconds*).

Press

Display/Comments

a) 2 [1/x] [lnx] [+/−] [÷]
   1.36 [EE↓] 11 [+/−] [=]

5.0967 10   seconds =
half-life (Check this out —
that's about 1600 years!)
Now to find number of atoms
left in a sample after 2
years, just convert 2 years
to seconds:

b) 2 [×] 365 [×] 24 [×] 60 [×]
   60 [=]

6.3072 07   or 63072000 seconds in 2 years.
Note: [INV] [lnx] is equivalent to
e^x

[×] 1.36 [+/−] [EE↓] 11 [+/−]
[=] [INV] [lnx]

9.9914 -01
Answer 99.914%, almost all
of it is left.

SECURING PHYSICS AND CHEMISTRY
Astronomy —
Universal Gravitation

It took man centuries just to write the laws which describe the effects of gravity. Of all natural phenomena, gravity — the fact that everything attracts everything else — is one of the most interesting. Gravity is also one of the most elusive phenomena to explain. All we really know about gravity are its effects. We know little about its cause. The gravitational force between two objects is given by:

$$F = G\frac{m_1 m_2}{R^2},$$ where m_1 and m_2 are the masses of each object, R the distance between their centers, and G the universal gravitation constant:
$$G = 6.6732 \times 10^{-11} \; (N - m^2/kg^2)$$

Example:
a) What acceleration due to gravity does the moon experience toward the earth? b) With what linear velocity (relative to the earth) does the moon travel in its orbit?

Solution: a) *Newton's Law* states:

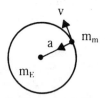

$$F = ma$$

Here:

$$F = \frac{G\, m_E m_m}{R^2} = m_m a$$

$$\text{or } \frac{Gm_E}{R^2} = a$$

b) The acceleration of the moon is *centripetal,* toward the center of the earth, and we can compute:

$$a = \frac{v^2}{R}; \text{ so } v = \sqrt{aR}$$

$$m_E = 5.98 \times 10^{24} \text{ kg,}$$
$$R = 3.80 \times 10^8 \text{ m}$$

Press

a)
6.6732 [EE↓] 11 [+/−] [X]
5.98 [EE↓] 24 [÷]
3.80 [EE↓] 8 [x²] [=]

b)
[X] 3.80 [EE↓] 8 [=] [√x]

Display/Comments

2.7636 −03
moon's acceleration:
.0027636 m/sec

1.0248 03   Speed in orbit:
1024.8 m/sec

Conservation of Momentum

Two bodies of mass m_1 and m_2 are moving through space at right angles to each other. They collide and stick together as shown below. Collisions such as this are called *completely inelastic* collisions. Find the direction and speed of the resulting object $(m_1 + m_2)$, if $m_1 = 60$ kg, $m_2 = 75$ kg, $V_1 = 30$ m/s and $V_2 = 25$ m/s.

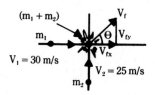

The conservation of momentum is a *vector relation* which in this case states: $m_1\mathbf{V}_1 + m_2\mathbf{V}_2 = (m_1 + m_2)\mathbf{V_f}$

In our case, since V_1 is only in the x direction, and V_2 is only in the y direction, the conservation of momentum gives us two scalar equations:

$$m_1 V_1 = (m_1 + m_2) V_{fx} \quad \text{or} \quad V_{fx} = \frac{m_1 V_1}{(m_1 + m_2)}$$

$$m_2 V_2 = (m_1 + m_2) V_{fy} \quad \text{or} \quad V_{fy} = \frac{m_2 V_2}{(m_1 + m_2)}$$

Once V_{fx} and V_{fy} are known, we can calculate the final speed V_f, and the angle Θ, from the equations:

$$V_f = \sqrt{V_{fx}^2 + V_{fy}^2} ; \quad \Theta = \tan^{-1} V_{fy}/V_{fx}.$$

On your calculator find V_{fx} and V_{fy} first:

Press

60 ⊠ 30 ÷ ⦅ 60	
⊞ 75 ⦆ ▭	
⟦STO⟧	
75 ⊠ 25 ÷ ⦅ 60	
⊞ 75 ⦆ ▭	
⟦x²⟧ ⊞ ⟦RCL⟧ ⟦x²⟧ ▭	
⟦√x⟧	
13.888889 ÷ ⟦RCL⟧ ▭	
⟦INV⟧ ⟦tan⟧	

Display/Comment

13.333333 m/sec $= V_{fx}$
Store this for use later.

13.888889 m/sec $= V_{fy}$.
Now to find V_f:
19.253026 m/sec = final speed. To find Θ:

46.16914°.

8-15

SECURING PHYSICS AND CHEMISTRY
Electrical Resistance and Ohm's Law

In your home, when different appliances are plugged into your wall outlets, they all get connected *in parallel,* across the house supply voltage. *Ohm's Law* relates the voltage (E) in the outlet, measured in volts (v), the total current (I) that will flow, measured in amperes (a), and the total resistance (R), measured in ohms (Ω), of the appliances:

Ohm's Law states: $E = I \times R$.

Resistances in parallel add according to the equation:

$$\frac{1}{R_t} = \frac{1}{R_1} + \frac{1}{R_2} + \frac{1}{R_3} + \text{etc.}$$

Example:
In your house you plug in 5 appliances having resistances of 5Ω, 12Ω, 17Ω, 23Ω, and 49Ω. What is the total resistance (R_t) of all these appliances when connected in parallel?

If these appliances were all turned on, how much current would they draw?
Assume the supply voltage is 115v.

Press	Display/Comments
5 $\boxed{1/x}$ $\boxed{+}$ 12 $\boxed{1/x}$ $\boxed{+}$	
17 $\boxed{1/x}$ $\boxed{+}$ 23 $\boxed{1/x}$ $\boxed{+}$	
49 $\boxed{1/x}$ $\boxed{=}$ $\boxed{1/x}$	**2.4627916** Ω This is the total resistance of the appliances:
$\boxed{STO}$	Store it.
115 $\boxed{\div}$ $\boxed{RCL}$ $\boxed{=}$	**46.694978** amperes.

If all these appliances were left on all day for a month (31 days), what would your electric bill be at 4¢ per kilowatt-hour? (Power in Watts = Volts × Amps.)

Answer: around $160.

SECURING PHYSICS AND CHEMISTRY
Gas Laws

A driver puts 20 N/cm² pressure in each tire of a car in
Death Valley (temperature = 35° C or 308° K). He then drives to
the top of Pike's Peak (temperature = 0° C or 273° K).
What is the pressure in each tire on Pike's Peak, assuming
the tire has stiff enough walls to prevent any change in its
volume?

Formula: $\dfrac{P_1}{T_1} = \dfrac{P_2}{T_2}$ $(T_1, T_2 \text{ in } ° K)$

Equation: $\dfrac{20}{308} = \dfrac{P_2}{273}$ or $P_2 = 273 \times \dfrac{20}{308}$

Press   **Display/Comments**

273 ☒ 20 ÷   P =
308 ☲   **17.727273**   N/cm² =
                    new pressure.

Actually, the tire walls would not retain constant volume with
the change in temperature and pressure. In actual cases, the
formula would be:

$$\frac{P_1 V_1}{T_1} = \frac{P_2 V_2}{T_2}$$

which utilizes the change in volume.

SECURING PHYSICS AND CHEMISTRY
Keying into Avogadro's Number

Some of the basic formulas and definitions in chemistry involve handling very large or small numbers. Your calculator can help keep accurate tabs on the arithmetic while you concentrate on the chem. A case in point: problems that involve *Avogadro's number.*

Examine the following definitions:
1 mole of a substance is an amount equal to its molecular weight in grams. Avogadro's number is the number of molecules in a mole of any substance, and equals 6.02217×10^{23}. At standard conditions (STP), 1 mole of any gas occupies 22.414 liters of volume.

A typical example:
How many a) moles and
b) molecules are there in 50 grams of SO_3 gas?
c) What's its volume at STP?

Solution:

a) # of moles $= \dfrac{\text{mass of gas}}{\text{Atomic weight of } SO_3}$

(a look in the periodic table in the Appendix will tell you the atomic weights of the various elements)

$$\text{\# of moles} = \frac{50}{32.064 + 3(15.9994)}$$

b) #of molecules = # of moles $\times$ Avogadro's number
c) Volume (STP) = # of moles $\times$ 22.414 liters/mole

Press	Display/Comments
50 $\div$ $($ 32.064 $+$ $($	a)
3 $\times$ 15.9994 $)$ $)$ $=$ STO	**0.62451444** number of moles
	b)
$\times$ 6.02217 EE⁺ 23 $=$	**3.7609 23** number of molecules: 3.7609×10^{23}.
	c)
RCL $\times$ 22.414 $=$	**1.3998 01** volume is 13.998 liters.

Amadeo Avogadro (1776-1856) was an Italian physicist who sought to reconcile findings by Dalton and Gay-Lussac and proposed that at equal temperatures and pressures, equal volumes of gases have the same number of molecules.

SECURING PHYSICS AND CHEMISTRY
Density-Volume

Density is the measure of how much mass per unit volume a substance has. Density × volume = mass.

Example:

Gold has a density of 19.28 gm/cm³, and an atomic weight of 196.967. If you have a cubic piece 5mm on a side, find:
a) the mass of the cube
b) the number of atoms in the cube
c) the mass of 1 atom of gold
d) the average volume of an atom of gold

Solution:

a) mass of cube = density × volume

b) # of atoms = $\dfrac{\text{mass of cube}}{\text{atomic weight}}$ × Avogadro's number

c) mass of one atom = $\dfrac{\text{mass of cube}}{\text{number of atoms in cube}}$

d) volume of atom = $\dfrac{\text{volume of cube}}{\text{number of atoms in cube}}$

Press

a)
19.28 $\boxed{\times}$ $\boxed{(}$ .5 $\boxed{y^x}$ 3
$\boxed{)}$ $\boxed{=}$

b) $\boxed{\div}$ 196.967 $\boxed{\times}$
6.02217 $\boxed{\text{EE↓}}$ 23 $\boxed{=}$
$\boxed{\text{STO}}$

c) 2.41 $\boxed{\div}$ $\boxed{\text{RCL}}$ $\boxed{=}$

d) .5 $\boxed{y^x}$ 3 $\boxed{=}$ $\boxed{\div}$
7.3685 $\boxed{\text{EE↓}}$ 21 $\boxed{=}$

Display/Comments

(5mm = .5cm)
2.41   total mass in grams

7.3685   21   Number of atoms =
7.4 × 10²¹

3.2707 −22   Mass of one
atom = 3.27 × 10⁻²²gm

1.6964 −23   Volume of one
atom = 1.6964 × 10⁻²³cm³

SECURING PHYSICS AND CHEMISTRY
Formula Determination

Using your calculator to help you with trials and estimates —
you can determine chemical formulas from analysis results.

Here's an example: What is the formula of calcium pyrophosphate
if it's found that it is:

    25.3% calcium
    39.2% phosphorus and
    35.5% oxygen?

Solution:

If you assume that you had 100 grams of the compound then:

    a) Decimal percent × 100g ÷ atomic weight = Relative amount
       (RA), in moles.
    b) (RA for any atom) ÷ (Smallest RA) = Ratio value.

Look at the periodic table in the appendix for the atomic
weights of the elements:

    Ca = 40.08
    P = 30.9738
    O = 15.9994

Press	Display/Comments	
25.3 ÷ 40.08 =	**0.63123752**	RA for calcium in moles.
39.2 ÷ 30.9738 =	**1.2655858**	RA for phosphorus in moles.
35.5 ÷ 15.9994 =	**2.2188332**	RA for oxygen in moles.

Now, calcium has the smallest RA — so divide each of the other RA's by it, and the ratio value for calcium is taken to be 1.

Press	Display/Comments	
.63123752 STO 1.2655858 ÷ RCL =	**2.0049280**	2 is the ratio value for phosphorus
2.2188332 ÷ RCL =	**3.5150528**	3.5 is the ratio value for oxygen

So using these ratio values, you'd find the formula for this
compound to be $Ca_1 P_2 O_{3.5}$. Normally, formulas should include
ratio values expressed as whole numbers — so you would double
these values to find the final formula: $Ca_2 P_4 O_7$.

SECURING PHYSICS AND CHEMISTRY
Keys Into Quantitative Analysis

A balanced equation for a chemical reaction provides you with a convenient way to calculate the mass relationships in a reaction. The ratio for any two of the substances in the reaction are related:

$$\frac{\text{mass of substance 1 (grams)}}{\substack{\text{gram molecular weight of} \\ \text{substance 1 involved in reaction}}} = \frac{\text{mass of substance 2 (grams)}}{\substack{\text{gram molecular weight of} \\ \text{substance 2 involved in reaction}}}$$

Example:
The equation for a reaction is:

$$Na_2CO_3 + 2HNO_3 \rightarrow 2NaNO_3 + H_2O + CO_2.$$

If 10 grams of Na_2CO_3 is consumed in this reaction, how much $NaNO_3$, H_2O, $+ CO_2$ are produced?

Solution: By looking up atomic weights in the *Appendix* (and adding) you can calculate the molecular weights:
$Na_2CO_3 = 105.9888$
$NaNO_3 = 84.9947$
$H_2O = 18.0154$
$CO_2 = 44.0098$

$$\frac{10 \text{ grams } (Na_2CO_3)}{105.9888} = \frac{\text{Mass of } NaNO_3}{2(84.9947)}$$

$$\frac{10 \ (Na_2CO_3)}{105.9888} = \frac{\text{Mass of } H_2O}{18.0154}$$

$$\frac{10 \ (Na_2CO_3)}{105.9888} = \frac{\text{Mass of } CO_2}{44.0098}$$

Press | **Display/Comments**

10 ÷ 105.9888 = STO
× 2 × 84.9947 =   **16.03843**   grams of $NaNO_3$
RCL × 18.0154 =   **1.6997456**   grams of H_2O
RCL × 44.0098 =   **4.1523067**   grams of CO_2

Antoine LaVoisier (1743-1794), known as the father of modern chemistry, was guillotined during the French Revolution for being an investor in a tax-collection company.

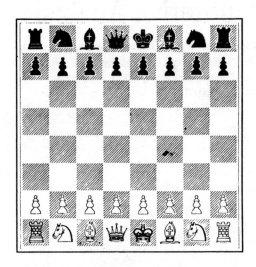

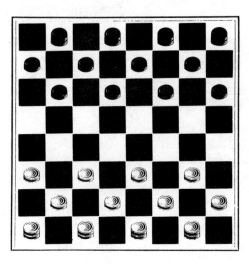

CLOSING ON PUZZLES AND GAMES
Introduction

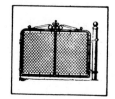

The first time someone picks up a handheld calculator, what happens? Do they immediately balance a checkbook? Calculate a best unit price? Do a science problem? No way! They *play* with it, that's what they do!

And well they should — because the handheld calculator, in addition to being a powerful tool, is also a great toy! Toddlers enjoy pressing the keys and watching the display light up at their command. Adults appreciate the "heft" of the little devices — packed with technological marvels, yet portable and rugged enough to tote everywhere. Nearly everybody loves watching the little things gobble up problems like 96385274 $\boxed{\div}$ 12345678 $\boxed{=}$. They do in a split second what might take us a half hour of pure drudgery. This feeling is one reason the calculator is making such an impact on the way we do mathematics today. With the arithmetic quickly and accurately handled on the calculator, we are freer to focus attention on the relationships — on the "how to" part of solving problems, and on the fun side of the world of numbers.

The following chapter is devoted to uses for the calculator that are primarily "recreational". All of them have their utilitarian or educational side, too. We hope you'll have fun exploring with these activities, and that they may help spark some of your own!

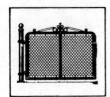

CLOSING ON PUZZLES AND GAMES
Numbers, Life, the Universe, and You!

With your calculator, you can explore and get the "feel" of some of the numbers in the world around you. Here are some random questions with interesting answers you can calculate. Then think up a few of your own!

Life Questions:

● How many times has your heart beat since you were born?

Solution: Get a watch and check your pulse.
Pulse rate (beats/min) ✕ 60 ✕ 24 ✕ 365.25 ✕ (your age) = # of beats.

● How many Saturday nights are there until you're 100? (Assume a long life!)

Solution: (100 − your age) ✕ 52 =
Ever thought about that? Does the number seem large or small to you?

● How much air do you breathe while you're alive?

Solution: Again assume you'll live to be 100! (Your lungs breathe in about 1 pint = .47 liters at a time. Check your # of breaths per minute with a watch (that's tricky to do!). Then:
# of breaths/min ✕ .47 ✕ 60 ✕ 24 ✕ 365 ✕ 100 = .

Astronomical Problems:

● Here's a table with some facts about our solar system. Your calculator can help you come up with some answers to questions about the planets:

Planet	Mercury	Venus	Earth	Mars	Jupiter	Saturn	Uranus	Neptune	Pluto
Mean diameter (km)	5,000	12,400	12,742	6,870	139,760	115,100	51,000	50,000	12,700(?)
Earth diameter	0.39	.973	1.00	.532	10.97	9.03	4.00	3.90	.46
Surface gravity as a function of Earth's	.27	.86	1.00	.37	2.64	1.17	.92	1.44	?

a) How much would you weigh on Saturn?

Solution:

Your weight $\boxed{\times}$ 1.17 $\boxed{=}$

b) If you drove around the equator (of the Earth) at 88 km/hour, how long would a round trip take? How about on Saturn? Mars?

Solution:

$\boxed{\pi}$ $\boxed{\times}$ diameter $\boxed{\div}$ 88 $\boxed{=}$ # of hours.

c) How many Earths could fit inside Saturn?

d) What others can you think up?

"Auto-Math":

● How many revolutions does a car's engine make in a mile? During its lifetime? (*Hint:* For most cars the engine runs at about 3500 rpm at 88 km/h).

● If there are about 130 million cars, buses and trucks in the U.S., how much do they weigh?

● If they all drive 5000 miles per year at 20 miles per gallon, how much gasoline will they need in a year?

● If there are 3.8 million miles of highway in the United States, how much is there for each car (if they were all "out" at once?).

● A steel belted radial tire is guaranteed for 40,000 miles (64,000 km). If the tread depth of the tire is 1 cm, and the average diameter of the tire 65 cm, how much rubber comes off the tire in 1 revolution?

(You actually "unwind" your tires in a ribbon several molecules thick!)

Inflation:

If the inflation rate stays at about 11.5%, how much will a $10.00 bag of groceries cost in 5 years? 10 years? 25 years? What about the cost of a $6000 car?

Solution: You can calculate the inflated rate by multiplying by 1.115 (100% + 11.5%).

Enter 1.115 as a multiplication consonant.

Now press the $\boxed{=}$ key once for each year of inflation you'd like to check. (After 25 years, the groceries cost $152!)

Problems with large and small numbers are around you all the time. They can come at you in advertising, get quoted in newspapers and magazines, or just arise in conversation. Remember — these can be easy and fun to handle on keys!

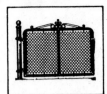

CLOSING ON PUZZLES AND GAMES
Hexagon 38

Your calculator and some logical thinking make this puzzle fun. Fill in each hexagon below with one of the whole numbers from 1 to 19, in such a way that all the numbers along any straight line add up to 38. (Don't use any of the numbers between 1 and 19 more than once.) A few have been put in to help out.

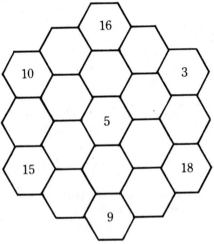

One Possible Solution to Hexagon 38:

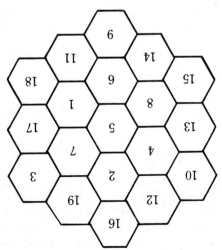

CLOSING ON PUZZLES AND GAMES
Days of
Your Life

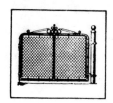

It's fun to use your calculator as a tallier of numbers that are often too large, small, or tedious to be routinely done on pencil and paper. One such number is the *exact* number of days you've been alive. With this number and a little "Biorhythm" theory you can see if you're "calculated" to have a good or bad day (see following section).

Here's how to calculate the exact number of days you've been alive:

● Enter your age, press ⊠ 365 ⊟ and store this: STO .
● Add the number of leap days you've been alive. (Just enter the number of leap days and press SUM .) The chart below will help you count the leap years:

> *Leap Year Chart:*
> (*Note:* If you were born in a leap year *before* Feb 29, count that year. If this is a leap year after Feb 29, count this year.)
>
> 1904 08 12 16 20 24 28 32 36 40 44 48 52 56 60 64 68 72 76 80 84 88

● add 1 day for your last birthday SUM .
● add the number of days since your last birthday SUM .

Note: If this is a leap year, be sure *not* to count Feb 29 this time — you should have already counted it in the leap day calculation above.

For those of you having trouble with "30 days hath September..." here's a chart of the number of days per month:

Jan	31	April	30	July	31	Oct	31
Feb	28	May	31	Aug	31	Nov	30
March	31	June	30	Sept	30	Dec	31

The memory now contains the exact number of days you've been alive. (You may want to write this down so you'll have it for future checks.) With this information you can now check out your "Biorhythm" condition — the next section shows you how!

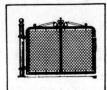

CLOSING ON PUZZLES AND GAMES
Fun with Biorhythm

The previous page shows how to use your calculator to quickly tally the exact number of days you've been alive. Once you have this number stored in memory, you can check out your "Biorhythm" picture as follows.

The Theory of Biorhythms states that there are 3 "cycles" to your life, which started on the day you were born:
The Physical Cycle: 23 days long
The Emotional Cycle: 28 days long
The Intellectual Cycle: 33 days long

You can check each of these — with the aid of the bio-rhythm chart included. The first half of each cycle are said to be "up" days, the last half "down" days. Days where a cycle curve is crossing the horizontal are said to be "critical days".

To check your "physical" cycle:
Press $\boxed{\text{RCL}}$ $\boxed{\div}$ 23 and $\boxed{=}$. From this result *subtract* the number to the left of the decimal point (the "whole number part"). Then, press $\boxed{=}$ $\boxed{\times}$ 23 $\boxed{=}$.

This result is the number of days you are "into" your current physical cycle. Look this number up on the center line of the chart, and then locate the position of the "Physical" cycle curve with respect to it. (Up above for good "awake" day, down for less active day.)

To check your "emotional" cycle:
Press $\boxed{\text{RCL}}$ $\boxed{\div}$ 28 $\boxed{=}$. From this result subtract the number to the left of the decimal. Press $\boxed{=}$ $\boxed{\times}$ 28 $\boxed{=}$.

This is the number of days you are now into your "emotional" or "sensitivity" cycle. Locate this number on the chart and find the position of the emotional cycle line.
(Up for good day — down for "the blues".)

To check your "intellectual cycle:

Press <kbd>RCL</kbd> <kbd>÷</kbd> 33 <kbd>=</kbd> . Subtract the number to the left of the decimal.

Press <kbd>=</kbd> <kbd>X</kbd> 33 <kbd>=</kbd> .

This is the number of days you are now into your "intellectual" cycle. Locate it on the chart and note the position of the "intellectual" cycle line. (Up for bright day, down for "forgetful" day.)

Note: According to the Biorhythm theory, cycle curves are crossing the horizontal line "critical days". Have a good day!

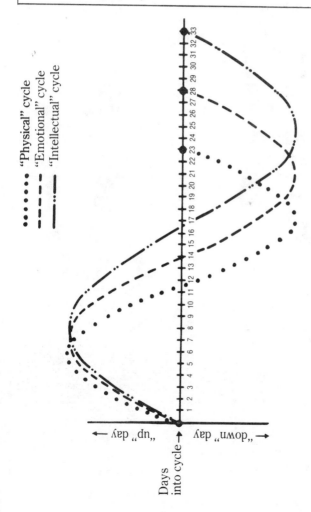

"Physical" cycle
"Emotional" cycle
"Intellectual" cycle

← "up" day

"down" day →

Days into cycle

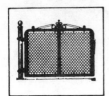

CLOSING ON PUZZLES AND GAMES
For Four 4's

Here's a brain teaser! Can you (with the help of your calculator, as needed) "build" all the whole numbers between 1 and 100 using only four 4's? Use only the

$\boxed{+}$ $\boxed{-}$ $\boxed{\times}$ $\boxed{\div}$ $\boxed{(}$ $\boxed{)}$ $\boxed{\cdot}$ $\boxed{x^2}$ $\boxed{=}$ and $\boxed{4}$

keys on your calculator. $4! = 4 \times 3 \times 2 \times 1$ is allowed, along with the repeating decimal $4(\dot{4} = .4444 \ldots)$. The first 8 are shown below. (All the whole numbers up to 119 have been "built" with just four 4's — how many can you find?)

$$1 = \frac{44}{44}$$

$$2 = \frac{4}{4} + \frac{4}{4}$$

$$3 = (4 + 4 + 4) \div 4$$

$$4 = (4! - 4 - 4) \div 4$$

$$5 = \frac{4 \times 4 + 4}{4}$$

$$6 = 4 + \frac{4 + 4}{4}$$

$$7 = 4 + 4 - \frac{4}{4}$$

$$8 = 4 + 4 + 4 - 4 .$$

CLOSING ON PUZZLES AND GAMES
Magicalc

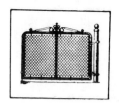

Amaze your friends with this (old, tried and true) mathematical trick — on keys! Hand a buddy your calculator and have him or her key in a favorite 3 digit number. Then have your friend:

a) Repeat the digits — making a 6 digit number (while doing this you can be playing Swami, Mr. Moto, the Great Zomboni, etc. for "effect").

b) Say that your magical power tells you that the number is divisible by 13. Have your friend hit ⎡÷⎤ 13 ⎡=⎤ . (Your friend will gasp — right! No remainder.)

c) Now you "feel" the result is divisible by 11: Have your friend key in ⎡÷⎤ 11 ⎡=⎤ . Once again you're right.

d) Now that you've gone through divisions by "unlucky" 13, and magic number 11 — you make a final suggestion; have your friend key in ⎡÷⎤ 7 ⎡=⎤ .
        SHAZAM!!

Back comes the original number — unharmed after all those divisions. (Be gracious about accepting applause.)

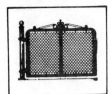

CLOSING ON PUZZLES AND GAMES
Gotcha!

Gotcha is a calculator game for 2 or more players that can be played anywhere you've got your calculator (in your car, while camping, etc.). Two or more can play.

Player 1 enters 50 into the display, and then secretly presses one of the operation keys $+$, $-$, $\times$, $\div$ or y^x . He or she then gives the calculator to the next player.

Player 2 then must enter any number (except 1), and then presses $=$.

If the display then displays a negative number, a number over 200, or "Error", player 2 loses and must leave the game.

If the display shows a number between 0 and 200, player 2 secretly presses $+$, $-$, $\times$, $\div$ or y^x , and passes the calculator, and the game goes on.

The game is over when only one player is left — the winner!

CLOSING ON PUZZLES AND GAMES
Fantasy Trip

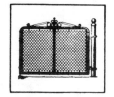

Travel! It's good for the soul. Your calculator can be
very handy for planning trips — no matter what the route,
or whatever way you're getting there. A little planning
can also save much hassle and help make a trip more enjoy-
able. (It's a lot easier to run out of gas (or money) on
your calculator, before you actually do on the highway!)

The following pages contain facts and tables that may help
you in planning or executing a trip (either a real one,
or one you'd just like to take sometime in the future).
If you're driving, you may want to keep the following in mind:

Metric Conversions:
1 mile per gallon = .425 km/liter
55 mph = 88.5 km/h

Formulas/Facts:
● If you drive 6 hours in a day you cover $6 \times 55 = 330$
miles/day.
● If your car's gas tank holds 20 gallons, at 20 miles per
gallon you'll go 400 miles on one tank of gas.
● Time to destination = distance $\div$ average speed
● Distance covered = speed $\times$ time
● Gasoline required = distance $\div$ mpg
The following tables show approximate distances between
selected cities, to help you in planning your trip.

	Anchorage, Alaska	Baltimore, Md.	Boston, Mass.	Chicago, Ill.	Cincinnati, Ohio	Columbus, Ohio	Dallas, Tex.	Denver, Colo.	Detroit, Mich.
Atlanta, Ga.	4317	642	1040	695	464	590	812	1407	718
Baltimore, Md.	4316		398	677	521	414	1373	1620	525
Boston, Mass.	4547	398		958	844	741	1762	1955	696
Charleston, W. Va.	4106	401	800	469	194	180	1066	1354	377
Chicago, Ill.	3639	677	958		296	307	936	1014	262
Cincinnati, Ohio	3930	521	844	296		111	948	1160	254
Colorado Springs, Colo.	3357	1627	1962	1023	1167	1233	726	69	1276
Columbia, S. C.	4437	485	880	798	527	583	1028	1588	725
Dallas, Tex.	4000	1373	1762	936	948	1052		785	1154
Denver, Colo.	3291	1620	1955	1014	1160	1226	785		1267
Des Moines, Iowa	3482	983	1273	324	567	613	718	690	604
Detroit, Mich.	3903	525	696	262	254	179	1154	1267	
Fresno, Calif.	3215	2780	3127	2214	2314	2386	1595	1210	2467
Hartford, Conn.	4482	297	105	893	743	640	1661	1866	662
Houston, Tex.	4249	1428	1817	1063	1037	1141	245	1027	1256
Indianapolis, Ind.	3822	592	914	189	107	173	887	1053	286
Jacksonville, Fla.	4629	769	1164	1011	780	840	995	1696	1019
Kansas City, Mo.	3596	1047	1394	496	581	653	512	601	734
Las Vegas, Nev.	3420	2421	2768	1824	1961	2027	1236	771	2077
Little Rock, Ark.	3988	1037	1426	629	612	716	336	955	822
Los Angeles, Calif.	3429	2626	2973	2075	2160	2232	1391	1102	2313
Louisville, Ky.	3936	609	956	301	96	201	842	1109	362
Macon, Ga.	4402	715	1114	779	548	674	836	1491	802
Memphis, Tenn.	4042	901	1290	531	481	585	472	1038	704
Miami, Fla.	4971	1141	1536	1349	1118	1206	1300	2010	1372
Milwaukee, Wisc.	3564	761	1042	86	380	391	1007	1039	368
Minn.-St. Paul, Minn.	3239	1077	1360	402	696	707	976	853	695
Mobile, Ala.	4405	993	1391	854	712	813	598	1367	966
Nashville, Tenn.	4070	697	1086	445	268	373	676	1157	520
New Orleans, La.	4402	1133	1522	915	821	922	502	1287	1069
New York, N. Y.	4450	187	211	806	633	530	1551	1756	616
Oklahoma City, Okla.	3789	1309	1656	791	837	915	211	614	1009
Omaha, Neb.	3405	1119	1409	460	676	741	656	554	713
Philadelphia, Pa.	4377	96	302	738	565	462	1469	1688	562
Phoenix, Ariz.	3693	2260	2607	1709	1794	1866	1004	795	1947
Pittsburgh, Pa.	4087	246	567	450	281	188	1225	1404	294
Pueblo, Colo.	3400	1629	1976	1057	1163	1235	683	112	1310
Raleigh, N. C.	4430	291	686	795	520	526	1195	1665	723
Reno, Nev.	2999	2595	2887	1938	2149	2214	1682	1036	2191
Richmond, Va.	4385	138	533	749	502	492	1277	1662	618
San Antonio, Tex.	4222	1614	2003	1208	1191	1295	277	936	1401
San Diego, Calif.	3547	2591	2938	2040	2125	2197	1319	1120	2278
St. Louis, Mo.	3783	803	1150	285	331	409	651	851	529
Salt Lake City, Utah	3045	2064	2356	1407	1618	1683	1245	505	1660
San Francisco, Calif.	3107	2821	3113	2164	2375	2440	1785	1262	2417
Seattle, Wash.	2288	2691	2949	2016	2310	2321	2103	1344	2276
Tampa, Fla.	4769	957	1352	1146	915	1003	1074	1796	1169
Tulsa, Okla.	3791	1207	1554	689	735	813	252	681	907
Washington, D.C.	4320	38	436	685	519	413	1355	1620	510

MILEAGE CHART FOR SELECTED CITIES

Houston, Tex.	Indianapolis, Ind.	Jacksonville, Fla.	Las Vegas, Nev.	Los Angeles, Calif.	Louisville, Ky.	Memphis, Tenn.	Miami, Fla.	Milwaukee, Wisc.	
802	523	316	1971	2176	411	375	654	777	Atlanta, Ga.
1428	592	769	2421	2626	609	901	1141	761	Baltimore, Md.
1817	914	1164	2768	2973	956	1290	1536	1042	Boston, Mass.
1150	301	674	2141	2346	259	594	1046	553	Charleston, W. Va.
1063	189	1011	1824	2075	301	531	1349	86	Chicago, Ill.
1037	107	780	1961	2160	96	481	1118	380	Cincinnati, Ohio
966	1060	1661	801	1090	1096	1003	1975	1048	Colorado Springs, Colo.
1017	641	294	2187	2392	530	591	666	882	Columbia, S. C.
245	887	995	1236	1391	842	472	1300	1007	Dallas, Tex.
1027	1053	1696	771	1102	1109	1038	2010	1039	Denver, Colo.
955	460	1213	1500	1772	564	603	1543	349	Des Moines, Iowa
1256	286	1019	2077	2313	362	704	1372	368	Detroit, Mich.
1745	2213	2590	390	217	2241	1955	2895	2239	Fresno, Calif.
1716	813	1063	2667	2872	855	1189	1435	977	Hartford, Conn.
	989	951	1425	1529	926	556	1199	1139	Houston, Tex.
989		839	1854	2059	112	437	1177	273	Indianapolis, Ind.
951	839		2239	2386	727	658	352	1093	Jacksonville, Fla.
749	480	1108	1374	1579	508	450	1422	551	Kansas City, Mo.
1425	1854	2239		282	1882	1596	2536	1849	Las Vegas, Nev.
439	555	794	1474	1679	506	136	1108	705	Little Rock, Ark.
1529	2059	2386	282		2087	1801	2691	2121	Los Angeles, Calif.
926	112	727	1882	2087		370	1065	385	Louisville, Ky.
823	607	243	2053	2227	495	457	576	861	Macon, Ga.
556	437	658	1596	1801	370		972	607	Memphis, Tenn.
1199	1177	352	2536	2691	1065	972		1431	Miami, Fla.
1139	273	1093	1849	2121	385	607	1431		Milwaukee, Wisc.
1213	589	1382	1617	1899	701	825	1736	342	Minn.-St. Paul, Minn.
516	713	435	1834	1989	606	362	712	930	Mobile, Ala.
760	285	559	1800	2005	175	204	904	527	Nashville, Tenn.
381	796	573	1738	1887	711	393	859	991	New Orleans, La.
1612	714	967	2557	2762	745	1079	1325	890	New York, N. Y.
460	739	1123	1133	1338	764	463	1435	862	Oklahoma City, Okla.
893	574	1297	1364	1636	673	642	1614	485	Omaha, Neb.
1524	641	879	2489	2694	677	997	1234	822	Philadelphia, Pa.
1147	1696	1991	290	387	1721	1435	2304	1764	Phoenix, Ariz.
1311	353	922	2205	2410	393	753	1221	534	Pittsburgh, Pa.
923	1062	1626	799	1056	1090	960	1932	1082	Pueblo, Colo.
1185	627	492	2322	2527	556	726	851	879	Raleigh, N. C.
1876	2042	2675	446	459	2138	2034	2982	1963	Reno, Nev.
1305	612	629	2401	2606	567	805	1003	833	Richmond, Va.
202	1134	1102	1260	1357	1083	713	1401	1284	San Antonio, Tex.
1481	2049	2322	331	121	2052	1766	2619	2095	San Diego, Calif.
837	236	863	1624	1829	258	277	1202	356	St. Louis, Mo.
1437	1513	2195	443	725	1607	1535	2507	1432	Salt Lake City, Utah
1925	2268	2747	580	378	2364	2145	3085	2189	San Francisco, Calif.
2293	2184	2949	1148	1130	2315	2299	3271	1940	Seattle, Wash.
1023	974	191	2310	2465	862	758	254	1228	Tampa, Fla.
507	673	1068	1240	1445	662	402	1374	760	Tulsa, Okla.
1389	569	742	2421	2626	601	863	1110	769	Washington, D.C.

	Minn.-St. Paul, Minn.	Nashville, Tenn.	New Orleans, La.	New York, N. Y.	Oklahoma City, Okla.	Omaha, Neb.	Philadelphia, Pa.	Phoenix, Ariz.	Pittsburgh, Pa.
Atlanta, Ga.	1082	236	498	829	838	996	738	1810	730
Baltimore, Md.	1077	697	1133	187	1309	1119	96	2260	246
Boston, Mass.	1360	1086	1522	211	1656	1409	302	2607	567
Charleston, W. Va.	869	404	923	536	1023	870	501	1980	231
Chicago, Ill.	402	445	915	806	791	460	738	1709	450
Cincinnati, Ohio	696	268	821	633	837	676	595	1794	281
Colorado Springs, Colo.	928	1144	1228	1763	572	597	1695	762	1411
Columbia, S. C.	1198	461	697	669	1054	1234	578	2026	634
Dallas, Tex.	976	676	502	1551	211	656	1469	1004	1225
Denver, Colo.	853	1157	1287	1756	614	554	1688	795	1404
Des Moines, Iowa	258	647	977	1112	551	136	1044	1418	756
Detroit, Mich.	695	520	1069	616	1009	713	562	1947	294
Fresno, Calif.	2007	2159	2097	2916	1492	1754	2848	603	2564
Hartford, Conn.	1293	985	1420	113	1561	1345	210	2518	472
Houston, Tex.	1213	760	381	1612	460	893	1524	1147	1311
Indianapolis, Ind.	589	285	796	714	739	574	641	1696	353
Jacksonville, Fla.	1382	509	573	967	1123	1297	879	1991	922
Kansas City, Mo.	464	576	806	1197	346	192	1115	1213	831
Las Vegas, Nev.	1617	1800	1738	2557	1133	1364	2489	290	2207
Little Rock, Ark.	820	340	450	1215	341	579	1133	1313	889
Los Angeles, Calif.	1899	2005	1887	2762	1338	1636	2694	387	2410
Louisville, Ky.	701	175	711	745	764	673	677	1721	393
Macon, Ga.	1166	320	503	863	920	1080	815	1840	783
Memphis, Tenn.	825	204	393	1079	463	642	997	1435	753
Miami, Fla.	1736	904	859	1325	1435	1614	1234	2304	1221
Milwaukee, Wisc.	342	527	991	890	862	485	822	1764	534
Minn.-St. Paul, Minn.		832	1218	1206	789	383	1138	1607	850
Mobile, Ala.	1171	425	147	1180	753	1004	1089	1602	979
Nashville, Tenn.	832		525	875	667	746	793	1639	563
New Orleans, La.	1218	525		1311	680	994	1229	1500	1088
New York, N. Y.	1206	875	1311		1445	1248	96	2396	356
Oklahoma City, Okla.	789	667	680	1445		452	1377	972	1093
Omaha, Neb.	383	746	994	1248	452		1180	1289	892
Philadelphia, Pa.	1138	793	1229	96	1377	1180		2328	288
Phoenix, Ariz.	1607	1639	1500	2396	972	1289	2328		2044
Pittsburgh, Pa.	850	563	1088	356	1093	892	288	2044	
Pueblo, Colo.	970	1117	1185	1765	529	639	1697	728	1413
Raleigh, N. C.	1195	522	881	475	1189	1196	384	2161	493
Reno, Nev.	1731	2186	2184	2724	1579	1476	2656	736	2368
Richmond, Va.	1149	634	1007	322	1268	1186	231	2240	339
San Antonio, Tex.	1252	917	560	1792	463	944	1710	970	1466
San Diego, Calif.	1932	1970	1815	2727	1303	1639	2659	358	2375
St. Louis, Mo.	548	324	670	939	506	440	871	1463	587
Salt Lake City, Utah	1200	1655	1747	2193	1104	945	2125	649	1837
San Francisco, Calif.	1957	2349	2287	2950	1682	1702	2882	793	2594
Seattle, Wash.	1615	2403	2605	2820	1955	1657	2752	1438	2464
Tampa, Fla.	1533	701	633	1141	1221	1400	1050	2078	1034
Tulsa, Okla.	716	606	681	1343	101	405	1275	1079	991
Washington, D.C.	1085	659	1095	225	1309	1125	134	2260	236

Reno, Nev.	Richmond, Va.	St. Louis, Mo.	Salt Lake City, Utah	San Antonio, Tex.	San Francisco, Calif.	San Diego, Calif.	Seattle, Wash.	Washington, D. C.	
2409	534	556	1905	1004	2520	2131	2653	604	Atlanta, Ga.
2595	138	803	2064	1614	2821	2591	2691	38	Baltimore, Md.
2887	533	1150	2356	2003	3113	2938	2949	436	Boston, Mass.
2343	308	517	1812	1307	2569	2311	2483	347	Charleston, W. Va.
1938	749	285	1407	1208	2174	2040	2016	685	Chicago, Ill.
2149	502	331	1618	1191	2375	2125	2310	519	Cincinnati, Ohio
1077	1663	838	549	869	1295	1087	1407	1627	Colorado Springs, Colo.
2617	363	785	2086	1219	2736	2347	2812	454	Columbia, S. C.
1682	1277	651	1245	277	1785	1319	2103	1355	Dallas, Tex.
1036	1662	851	505	936	1262	1120	1344	1620	Denver, Colo.
1614	1055	343	1083	995	1840	1749	1764	991	Des Moines, Iowa
2191	618	529	1660	1401	2417	2278	2276	510	Detroit, Mich.
304	2760	1983	819	1573	190	338	913	2780	Fresno, Calif.
2818	437	1058	2289	1915	3042	2871	2900	336	Hartford, Conn.
1876	1305	837	1437	202	1925	1481	2293	1389	Houston, Tex.
2042	612	236	1513	1134	2268	2049	2184	569	Indianapolis, Ind.
2675	629	863	2195	1102	2747	2322	2949	742	Jacksonville, Fla.
1630	1087	250	1099	779	1856	1566	1849	1047	Kansas City, Mo.
446	2401	1624	443	1260	580	331	1148	2421	Las Vegas, Nev.
1920	941	378	1445	612	2023	1644	2236	999	Little Rock, Ark.
459	2606	1829	725	1357	378	121	1130	2626	Los Angeles, Calif.
2138	567	258	1607	1083	2364	2052	2315	601	Louisville, Ky.
2491	587	640	1989	1025	2602	2155	2737	648	Macon, Ga.
2034	805	277	1535	713	2145	1766	2299	863	Memphis, Tenn.
2982	1003	1202	2507	1401	3085	2619	3271	1110	Miami, Fla.
1963	833	356	1432	1284	2189	2095	1940	769	Milwaukee, Wisc.
1731	1149	548	1200	1252	1957	1932	1615	1085	Minn.-St. Paul, Minn.
2280	860	623	1843	689	2383	1917	2661	955	Mobile, Ala.
2186	634	324	1655	917	2349	1970	2403	659	Nashville, Tenn.
2184	1007	670	1747	560	2287	1815	2605	1095	New Orleans, La.
2724	322	939	2193	1792	2950	2727	2820	225	New York, N. Y.
1579	1268	506	1104	463	1682	1303	1955	1309	Oklahoma City, Okla.
1476	1186	440	945	944	1702	1639	1657	1125	Omaha, Neb.
2656	231	871	2125	1710	2882	2659	2752	134	Philadelphia, Pa.
736	2240	1463	649	970	793	358	1438	2260	Phoenix, Ariz.
2368	339	587	1837	1466	2594	2375	2464	236	Pittsburgh, Pa.
1074	1657	832	575	826	1292	1053	1433	1629	Pueblo, Colo.
2669	153	814	2138	1387	2871	2492	2809	260	Raleigh, N. C.
	2650	1880	531	1706	226	552	708	2598	Reno, Nev.
2650		825	2119	1513	2876	2571	2763	102	Richmond, Va.
1706	1513	915	1318		1763	1305	2176	1576	San Antonio, Tex.
552	2571	1794	774	1305	497		1251	2591	San Diego, Calif.
1880	825		1349	915	2106	1794	2090	803	St. Louis, Mo.
531	2119	1349		1318	757	774	858	2067	Salt Lake City, Utah
226	2876	2106	757	1763		497	812	2824	San Francisco, Calif.
708	2763	2097	858	2176	812	1251		2699	Seattle, Wash.
2756	819	995	2293	1175	2859	2393	3057	926	Tampa, Fla.
1670	1207	404	1171	534	1789	1410	2007	1207	Tulsa, Okla.
2598	102	803	2067	1576	2824	2591	2699		Washington, D.C.

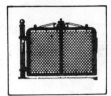

Flipit — Puzzles

By now everyone's realized that when you flip your calculator over — some of the numbers look like letters. Some numbers do a better job at this than others — but with a little imagination you can see that the following numbers correspond to the letters shown when the calculator is "flipped":

0 = o	5 = S
1 = I	6 = g *
2 = Z *	7 = L
3 = E	8 = B *
4 = h	9 = G *

*(These "letters" are often tougher to "see" — until you get used to them.)

Flipit Crossword

Across

1) (2689 + .954) × 2000 =

4) 2 × 7 =

5) (30 × 500 + 469) × 5 =

6) 315 × 100 + 73 =

8) 4 × 4 × 100 = √

9) 60 × 1000 − 2292 =

12) 34225 × 4 = √

13) 17 × 2 =

14) (300 + 79) × 1000 + 919 =

Down

1) 30 × 100 + 718 =

2) 175 × 100 × 2 + 9 =

3) 1753.5 × 2 =

4) 1 − .2266 =

7) (.4 − .0061) ÷ 3 =

10) 185 x² × 4 = √

11) 800 + 105 =

15) 1 − .3 =

Answers

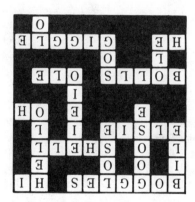

9-17

APPENDIX 1
Alphabetical Conversion Tables

Unless designated otherwise, the English measures of capacity are those used in the United States, and the units of weight and mass are avoirdupois units.

MULTIPLY	BY	TO OBTAIN
Acres	43560	Square feet
Acres	4047	Square meters
Acres	0.0016	Square miles
Acres	4840	Square yards
Acre feet	43560	Cubic feet
Acre feet	1233.48	Cubic meters
Atmospheres	76.0	Centimeters – mercury
Atmospheres	29.92	Inches – mercury
Atmospheres	14.70	Pounds/in.^{2}
Atmopsheres	1.058	Tons/ft.^{2}
Barrels – oil	42	Gallons – oil
Board feet	144	Cubic inches
British Thermal Units	777.6	Foot-pounds
British Thermal Units	3.927×10^{-4}	Horsepower-hours
British Thermal Units	2.928×10^{-4}	Kilowatt-hours
Btu/min	12.96	Foot-pounds/s
Btu/min	0.0236	Horsepower
Btu/min	17.57	Watts
Centares (Centiares)	1	Square meters
Centigrams	0.01	Grams
Centimeters	0.3937	Inches
Centimeters	0.01	Meters
Centimeters	10	Millimeters
Centimeters – mercury	0.0132	Atmospheres
Centimeters – mercury	0.4460	Feet – water (4° C)
Centimeters – mercury	136.0	Kilograms/m^2
Centimeters – mercury	27.85	Pounds/ft^2
Centimeters – mercury	0.1934	Pounds/in.^{2}
Centimeters/s	0.0328	Feet/s
Centimeters/s	0.036	Kilometers/h
Centimeters/s	0.6	Meters/min
Centimeters/s	0.0224	Miles/h
Centimeters/s	0.0004	Miles/min

MULTIPLY	BY	TO OBTAIN
Cubic centimeters	3.531×10^{-5}	Cubic feet
Cubic centimeters	.0610	Cubic inches
Cubic centimeters	1×10^{-6}	Cubic meters
Cubic centimeters	1.3079×10^{-6}	Cubic yards
Cubic centimeters	2.642×10^{-4}	Gallons
Cubic centimeters	0.0010	Liters
Cubic centimeters	0.0021	Pints (liq.)
Cubic centimeters	0.0011	Quarts (liq.)
Cubic feet	1728	Cubic inches
Cubic feet	0.0283	Cubic meters
Cubic feet	7.4805	Gallons
Cubic feet	28.32	Liters
Cubic feet	59.84	Pints (liq.)
Cubic feet	29.92	Quarts (liq.)
Cubic feet/min	0.1247	Gallons/s
Cubic feet/min	0.4719	Liters/s
Cubic feet/s	448.831	Gallons/min
Cubic inches	16.39	Cubic centimeters
Cubic inches	0.0005787	Cubic feet
Cubic inches	1.6387×10^{-5}	Cubic meters
Cubic inches	2.1433×10^{-5}	Cubic yards
Cubic inches	0.004329	Gallons
Cubic inches	0.0164	Liters
Cubic inches	0.0346	Pints (liq.)
Cubic inches	0.0173	Quarts (liq.)
Cubic meters	1×10^{6}	Cubic centimeters
Cubic meters	35.31	Cubic feet
Cubic meters	61023	Cubic inches
Cubic meters	1.308	Cubic yards
Cubic meters	264.2	Gallons
Cubic meters	1000	Liters
Cubic meters	2113	Pints (liq.)
Cubic meters	1057	Quarts (liq.)
Cubic yards	27	Cubic feet
Cubic yards	46.656	Cubic inches
Cubic yards	0.7645	Cubic meters
Cubic yards	202.0	Gallons
Cubic yards	764.5	Liters
Cubic yards	1616	Pints (liq.)
Cubic yards	807.9	Quarts (liq.)
Cubic yards/min	0.45	Cubic feet/s
Cubic yards/min	3.367	Gallons/s
Cubic yards/min	12.74	Liter/s

MULTIPLY	BY	TO OBTAIN
Degrees (angle)	60	Minutes
Degrees (angle)	0.0174	Radians
Degrees (angle)	3600	Seconds
Degree/s	0.1667	Revolutions/min
Degree/s	0.0028	Revolutions/s
Drams	27.34	Grains
Drams	0.0625	Ounces
Drams	1.7718	Grams
Fathoms	6	Feet
Feet	30.48	Centimeters
Feet	12	Inches
Feet	0.3048	Meters
Feet	0.3333	Yards
Feet — water (4° C)	0.8826	Inches — mercury
Feet — water	62.43	Pounds/ft^2
Feet/min	0.5080	Centimeters/s
Feet/min	0.0183	Kilometers/h
Feet/min	0.3048	Meters/min
Feet/min	0.0114	Miles/h
Feet/s	30.48	Centimeters/s
Feet/s	1.097	Kilometers/h
Feet/s	18.29	Meters/min
Feet/s	0.6818	Miles/h
Feet/s	0.0114	Miles/min
Foot-pounds	0.0013	British Thermal Un
Foot-pounds	5.0505 x 10^{-7}	Horsepower-hours
Foot-pounds	3.766 x 10^{-7}	Kilowatt-hours
Foot-pounds/min	0.0167	Foot-pounds/s
Foot-pounds/min	3.030 x 10^{-5}	Horsepower
Foot-pounds/min	2.2597 x 10^{-5}	Kilowatts
Gallons	3785	Cubic centimeters
Gallons	0.1337	Cubic feet
Gallons	231	Cubic inches
Gallons	0.0038	Cubic meters
Gallons	3.785	Liters
Gallons	8	Prints (liq.)
Gallons	4	Quarts (liq.)
Gallons, Imperial	1.2009	U.S. gallons
Gallons, U.S.	0.8327	Imperial gallons
Gallons — water	8.34	Pounds — water
Grams	980.7	Dynes
Grams	15.43	Grains
Grams	0.0353	Ounces

MULTIPLY	BY	TO OBTAIN
Grams	0.0322	Ounces (troy)
Grams	0.0022	Pounds
Grams/cm³	0.0361	Pounds/in.³
Hectares	2.471	Acres
Horsepower	42.44	Btu/min
Horsepower	33000	Foot-pounds/min
Horsepower	550	Foot-pounds/s
Horsepower	1.014	Horsepower (metric)
Horsepower	0.7457	Kilowatts
Horsepower-hours	0.7457	Kilowatt-hours
Inches	2.540	Centimeters
Inches — mercury	0.033	Atmospheres
Inches — mercury	345.3	Kilograms/m²
Inches — mercury	70.73	Pounds/ft²
Inches — water	0.0735	Inches — mercury
Kilograms	980665	Dynes
Kilograms	2.205	Pounds
Kilometers	3281	Feet
Kilometers	1000	Meters
Kilometers	0.6214	Miles
Kilometers	1094	Yards
Kilometers/h	54.68	Feet/min
Kilometers/h	0.5396	Knots
Kilowatts	56.82	Btu/min
Kilowatts	44253.7	Foot-pounds/min
Kilowatts	737.6	Foot-pounds/s
Kilowatts	1.341	Horsepower
Kilowatt-hours	3410	British Thermal Units

MULTIPLY	BY	TO OBTAIN
Kilowatt-hours	2.655×10^6	Foot-pounds
Kilowatt-hours	1.341	Horsepower-hours
Liters	0.0353	Cubic feet
Liters	61.02	Cubic inches
Liters	0.0010	Cubic meters
Liters	0.2642	Gallons
Liters	2.113	Pints (liq.)
Liters	1.057	Quarts (liq.)
Meters	3.281	Feet
Meters	39.37	Inches
Meters	0.001	Kilometers
Meters	1.094	Yards
Meters/min	3.281	Feet/min
Meters/min	0.06	Kilometers/h
Meters/min	0.0373	Miles/h
Meters/s	196.8	Feet/min
Meters/s	3.281	Feet/s
Meters/s	3.6	Kilometers/h
Meters/s	0.03728	Miles/min
Microns	1×10^6	Meters
Miles	5280	Feet
Miles	1.609	Kilometers
Miles	1760	Yards
Miles/h	44.70	Centimeters/s
Miles/h	88	Feet/min
Miles/h	1.467	Feet/s

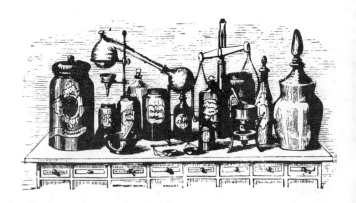

MULTIPLY	BY	TO OBTAIN
Miles/h	1.609	Kilometers/h
Miles/h	0.8690	Knots
Miles/h	26.82	Meters/min
Miles/min	2682	Centimeters/s
Miles/min	88	Feet/s
Miles/min	1.609	Kilometers/min
Miles/min	60	Miles/h
Milligrams	0.001	Grams
Milliliters	0.001	Liters
Millimeters	0.1	Centimeters
Millimeters	0.0394	Inches
Ounces	16	Drams
Ounces	437.5	Grains
Ounces	0.0625	Pounds
Ounces	0.9115	Ounces (troy)
Ounces	2.8349×10^{-5}	Tons (metric)
Ounces (troy)	1.0971	Ounces (avoir.)
Ounces (fluid)	1.805	Cubic inches
Ounces (fluid)	0.0296	Liters
Pounds	16	Ounces
Pounds	256	Drams
Pounds	7000	Grains
Pounds	0.0005	Tons (short)
Pounds	1.2153	Pounds (troy)
Pounds/in.^{3}	1728	Pounds/ft.^{3}
Pounds/ft.	1488	Kilograms/m
Pounds/in.	178.6	Grams/cm
Pounds/ft.^{2}	4.882	Kilograms/m^2
Pounds/in.^{2}	0.0680	Atmospheres
Pounds/in.^{2}	2.036	Inches – mercury
Quadrants (angle)	1.571	Radians
Quarts (liq.)	57.75	Cubic inches
Quintal, metric	220.46	Pounds
Radians	57.30	Degrees
Radians	3438	Minutes
Radians	0.637	Quadrants
Radians/s	9.549	Revolutions/min
Revolutions/s	360	Degrees/s
Revolutions/s	6.283	Radians/s
Revolutions/s	60	Revolutions/min
Seconds (angle)	4.8481×10^{-6}	Radians
Square centimeters	0.0011	Square feet
Square centimeters	0.1550	Square inches

MULTIPLY	BY	TO OBTAIN
Square centimeters	0.0001	Square meters
Square centimeters	100	Square millimeter
Square feet	2.2957×10^{-5}	Acres
Square feet	929.0	Square centimete
Square feet	144	Square inches
Square feet	0.0929	Square meters
Square feet	3.5870×10^{-8}	Square miles
Square feet	0.1111	Square yards
Square inches	6.452	Square centimete
Square inches	0.0069	Square feet
Square kilometers	247.1	Acres
Square kilometers	1.0764×10^{7}	Square feet
Square kilometers	1×10^{6}	Square meters
Square kilometers	0.3861	Square miles
Square kilometers	1.1960×10^{6}	Square yards
Square meters	10.76	Square feet
Square meters	1.1960	Square yards
Square miles	640	Acres
Square miles	2.590	Square kilometer
Square miles	3.0976×10^{6}	Square yards
Square millimeters	0.01	Square centimete
Square millimeters	0.0016	Square inches
Square yards	9	Square feet
Square yards	0.8361	Square meters
Square yards	3.2283×10^{-7}	Square miles
Tons (metric)	1000	Kilograms
Tons (metric)	2205	Pounds
Tons (short)	2000	Pounds
Tons (short)	0.89286	Tons (long)
Tons (short)	0.9072	Tons (metric)
Watts	0.0586	Btu(mean)/min
Watts	0.7377	Foot-pounds/s
Watts	0.0013	Horsepower
Watts	0.001	Kilowatts
Watt-hours	3.4144	British Thermal U
Watt-hours	2655	Foot-pounds
Watt-hours	0.00134	Horsepower-hou
Watt-hours	0.001	Kilowatt-hours
Yards	91.44	Centimeters
Yards	3	Feet
Yards	36	Inches
Yards	0.9144	Meters

Reference Tables

Table 1
Areas of Common Plane Figures

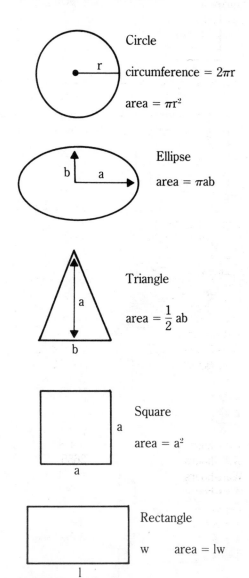

Circle

circumference $= 2\pi r$

area $= \pi r^2$

Ellipse

area $= \pi ab$

Triangle

area $= \dfrac{1}{2} ab$

Square

area $= a^2$

Rectangle

area $= lw$

Table 2
Areas and Volumes of Common Shapes

	(Surface) Area	Volume
Cube:	$6\,a^2$	a^3
Rectangular Prism	$2hw + 2hl + 2lw$	$1 \times w \times h$
Sphere	$4\pi r^2$	$\dfrac{4}{3}\pi r^3$
Cylinder	$2\pi rh + 2\pi r^2$	$\pi r^2 h$
Cone	$\pi r\sqrt{r^2 + h^2}$ ($+\pi r^2$ if you add the base)	$\dfrac{\pi r^2 h}{3}$

Table 3
Mathematical Expressions

Trigonometric Relations

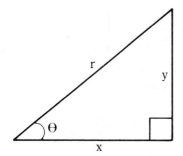

$$\sin \Theta = \frac{y}{r}$$

$$\cos \Theta = \frac{x}{r}$$

$$\tan \Theta = \frac{y}{x}$$

$$\sin^2 \Theta + \cos^2 \Theta = 1$$

$$e^{i\theta} = \cos \Theta + i \sin \Theta \qquad i = \sqrt{-1}$$

Law of Cosines

$$a^2 + b^2 - 2ab \cos \Theta = c^2$$

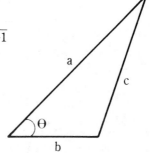

Laws of Exponents

$$a^x \times a^y = a^{x+y} \qquad \frac{1}{a^x} = a^{-x}$$

$$(ab)^x = a^x \times b^x \qquad \frac{a^x}{a^y} = a^{x-y}$$

$$(a^x)^y = a^{xy} \qquad a^0 = 1$$

Laws of Logarithms

$$Ln(y^x) = xLn\ y$$

$$Ln(ab) = Ln\ a + Ln\ b$$

$$Ln\left(\frac{a}{b}\right) = Ln\ a - Ln\ b$$

Here are a few fundamental identities that are frequently used in trigonometry. A and B represent any angles.

Reciprocal relations $\sin A = \dfrac{1}{\csc A}$, $\cos A = \dfrac{1}{\sec A}$, $\tan A = \dfrac{1}{\cot A}$

$\csc A = \dfrac{1}{\sin A}$, $\sec A = \dfrac{1}{\cos A}$, $\cot A = \dfrac{1}{\tan A}$

Product relations

$\sin A = \tan A \cos A$, $\cos A = \cot A \sin A$, $\tan A = \sin A \sec A$,
$\cot A = \cos A \csc A$, $\sec A = \csc A \tan A$, $\csc A = \sec A \cot A$

Pythagorean relations

$\sin^2 A + \cos^2 A = 1$, $1 + \tan^2 A = \sec^2 A$, $1 + \cot^2 A = \csc^2 A$

Angle-sum and angle-difference relations

$\sin (A \pm B) = \sin A \cos B \pm \cos A \sin B$
$\cos (A \pm B) = \cos A \cos B \mp \sin A \sin B$

$\tan (A \pm B) = \dfrac{\tan A \pm \tan B}{1 \mp \tan A \tan B}$, $\cot (A \pm B) = \dfrac{\cot B \cot A \mp 1}{\cot B \pm \cot A}$

$\sin (A + B) \sin (A - B) = \sin^2 A - \sin^2 B = \cos^2 B - \cos^2 A$
$\cos (A + B) \cos (A - B) = \cos^2 A - \sin^2 B = \cos^2 B - \sin^2 A$

Double-angle relations

$\sin 2A = 2 \sin A \cos A = \dfrac{2 \tan A}{1 + \tan^2 A}$

$\cos 2A = \cos^2 A - \sin^2 A = 2 \cos^2 A - 1 = 1 - 2 \sin^2 A = \dfrac{1 - \tan^2 A}{1 + \tan^2 A}$

$\tan 2A = \dfrac{2 \tan A}{1 - \tan^2 A}$, $\cot 2A = \dfrac{\cot^2 A - 1}{2 \cot A}$

Function-product relations

$\sin A \sin B = .5 \cos(A - B) - .5 \cos(A + B)$
$\cos A \cos B = .5 \cos(A - B) + .5 \cos(A + B)$
$\sin A \cos B = .5 \sin (A + B) + .5 \sin (A - B)$
$\cos A \sin B = .5 \sin (A + B) - .5 \sin (A - B)$

Function-sum and function-difference relations

$\sin A \pm \sin B = 2 \sin .5(A \pm B) \cos .5 (A \mp B)$
$\cos A + \cos B = 2 \cos .5(A + B) \cos .5 (A - B)$
$\cos A - \cos B = -2 \sin .5(A + B) \sin .5(A - B)$

$\tan A \pm \tan B = \dfrac{\sin (A \pm B)}{\cos A \cos B}$

Power relations

$\sin^2 A = .5 (1 - \cos 2A)$, $\sin^3 A = .25 (3 \sin A - \sin 3A)$,
$\sin^4 A = .125 (3 - 4 \cos 2A + \cos 4A)$, $\cos^2 A = .5(1 + \cos 2A)$,
$\cos^3 A = .25 (3 \cos A + \cos 3A)$, $\cos^4 A = .125(3 + 4\cos 2A + \cos 4A$

$\tan^2 A = \dfrac{1 - \cos 2A}{1 + \cos 2A}$, $\cot^2 A = \dfrac{1 + \cos 2A}{1 - \cos 2A}$

APPENDIX 3
Hyperbolic Functions

Solving problems involving hyperbolic functions uses the exponential ($\boxed{\text{INV}}$ $\boxed{\text{In}x}$) capability of your calculator.

Hyperbolic Sine (sinh) $x = 1/2(e^x - e^{-x}) = \dfrac{e^{2x} - 1}{2e^x}$

Hyperbolic Cosine (cosh) $x = 1/2(e^x + e^{-x}) = \dfrac{e^{2x} + 1}{2e^x}$

Hyperbolic Tangent (tanh) $x = \dfrac{e^x - e^{-x}}{e^x + e^{-x}} = \dfrac{e^{2x} - 1}{e^{2x} + 1}$

Example: tanh 2.99 = .99495511

Press	**Display/Comments**
2.99 $\boxed{\times}$	**2.99**
2 $\boxed{=}$	**5.98**
$\boxed{\text{INV}}$ $\boxed{\text{In}x}$ $\boxed{\text{STO}}$ $\boxed{-}$	**395.44037**
1 $\boxed{=}$ $\boxed{\div}$	**394.44037**
$\boxed{(}$ $\boxed{\text{RCL}}$ $\boxed{+}$	**395.44037**
1 $\boxed{)}$ $\boxed{=}$	**.99495511**

Inverse Hyperbolic Functions

$\sinh^{-1}x = \text{Ln}(x + \sqrt{x^2 + 1})$
$\cosh^{-1}x = \text{Ln}(x + \sqrt{x^2 - 1})$
$\tanh^{-1}x = 1/2\ \dot{\text{L}}\text{n}\left(\dfrac{1 + x}{1 - x}\right)$

Example: $\sinh^{-1}$ 86.213 = 5.1500018

Press	**Display/Comments**
86.213 $\boxed{+}$ $\boxed{(}$	**86.213**
$\boxed{x^2}$ $\boxed{+}$	**7432.6814**
1 $\boxed{)}$	**7433.6814**
$\boxed{\sqrt{x}}$	**86.218799**
$\boxed{=}$	**172.4318**
$\boxed{\text{In}x}$	**5.1500018**

Physical Constants

Constant	Symbol	Value	
Speed of Light	c	2.9979250	10^8m sec^{-1}
Electron Charge	e	1.6021917	10^{-19}C
Avogadro Number	N	6.022169	10^{26}k mole^{-1}
Electron Rest Mass	m_e	9.109558	10^{-31}kg
	m_e	5.485930	10^{-4}amu
Proton Rest Mass	M_p	1.672614	10^{-27}kg
	M_p	1.00727661	amu
Neutron Rest Mass	M_n	1.674920	10^{-27}kg
	M_n	1.00866520	amu
Atomic Mass Unit	amu	1.660531	10^{-27}kg
Electron Charge to Mass ratio	e/m_e	1.7588028	10^{11}C kg^{-1}
Planck Constant	h	6.626196	10^{-34}J-sec
Rydberg Constant	R_∞	1.09737312	10^7m^{-1}
Gas Constant	R_0	8.31434	10^3J-k mole^{-1}K^{-1}
Boltzmann Constant	k	1.380622	10^{-23}JK^{-1}
Gravitational Constant	G	6.6732	10^{-11}N-m^{2}kg^{-2}
Bohr Magneton	μ_B	9.274096	10^{-24}JT^{-1}
Electron Magnetic Moment	μ_e	9.284851	10^{-24}JT^{-1}
Proton Magnetic Moment	μ_p	1.4106203	10^{-26}JT^{-1}
Compton Wavelength of the Electron	λ_c	2.4263096	10^{-12}m
Compton Wavelength of the Proton	$\lambda_{c,p}$	1.3214409	10^{-15}m
Compton Wavelength of the Neutron	$\lambda_{c,n}$	1.3196217	10^{-15}m
Faraday Constant	F	9.648670	10^7C k mole^{-1}

APPENDIX 5
Periodic Table of the Elements

1a	2a	3b	4b	5b	6b	7b	8 — Group 8			1b	2b	3a	4a	5a	6a	7a	0	Orbit
1 H 1.008																	2 He 4.0026	K
3 Li 6.94	4 Be 9.01218											5 B 10.81	6 C 12.011	7 N 14.0067	8 O 15.9994	9 F 18.9994	10 Ne 20.17	K L
11 Na 22.9898	12 Mg 24.305											13 Al 26.9815	14 Si 28.086	15 P 30.9738	16 S 32.06	17 Cl 34.453	18 Ar 39.948	K L M
19 K 39.102	20 Ca 40.08	21 Sc 44.9559	22 Ti 47.90	23 V 50.941	24 Cr 51.996	25 Mn 54.9380	26 Fe 55.847	27 Co 58.9332	28 Ni 58.71	29 Cu 63.546	30 Zn 65.37	31 Ga 69.72	32 Ge 72.59	33 As 74.9216	34 Se 78.96	35 Br 79.904	36 Kr 83.80	L M N
37 Rb 85.467	38 Sr 87.62	39 Y 88.9059	40 Zr 91.22	41 Nb 92.9064	42 Mo 95.94	43 Tc 98.9062	44 Ru 101.07	45 Rh 102.9055	46 Pd 106.4	47 Ag 107.868	48 Cd 112.40	49 In 114.82	50 Sn 118.69	51 Sb 121.75	52 Te 127.60	53 I 126.9045	54 Xe 131.30	M N O
55 Cs 132.9055	56 Ba 137.34	57* La 138.905	72 Hf 178.49	73 Ta 180.947	74 W 183.85	75 Re 186.2	76 Os 190.2	77 Ir 192.22	78 Pt 195.09	79 Au 196.9665	80 Hg 200.59	81 Tl 204.37	82 Pb 207.2	83 Bi 208.9806	84 Po (209)	85 At (210)	86 Rn (222)	N O P
87 Fr (223)	88 Ra (226)	89** Ac (227)	104 —	105														O P Q

*Lanthanides														Orbit
58 Ce 140.12	59 Pr 140.907	60 Nd 144.24	61 Pm (145)	62 Sm 150.4	63 Eu 151.96	64 Gd 157.25	65 Tb 158.925	66 Dy 162.50	67 Ho 164.9303	68 Er 167.26	69 Tm 168.934	70 Yb 173.04	71 Lu 174.97	N O P

**Actinides														Orbit
90 Th 232.038	91 Pa 231.035	92 U 238.029	93 Np 237.048	94 Pu (244)	95 Am (243)	96 Cm (247)	97 Bk (247)	98 Cf (251)	99 Es (254)	100 Fm (257)	101 Md (256)	102 No (254)	103 Lr	O P Q

Numbers in parentheses are mass numbers of most stable isotope of that element.

Bibliography

BASIC CALCULATOR USAGE

Fundamental Mathematics Teacher's Guide. Calculator Math Fundamental Mathematics. Dallas, Texas: The Texas Instruments Education and Communications Center, 1976.

Immerzeel, George. *Ideas & Activities for Using Calculators in the Classroom.* Dansville, New York: The Instructor Publications, Inc., 1976.

Roberts, Edward M. *Fingertip Math.* Dallas, Texas: Texas Instruments, Inc., 1974.

Rudolph, William B., Claassen, A.D. *The Calculator Book.* Boston: Houghton Mifflin Company, 1976.

HOME MANAGEMENT

Bogart, L. Jean. *Nutrition and Physical Fitness.* Philadelphia: W.B. Saunders Co., 1960.

Langford, Francis G., Jr., Goe, William E. *Consumer Mathematics.* New York: Harcourt Brace Jovanovich, Inc., 1974.

Meyer, Robert. *Consumer and Business Mathematics.* Garden City, N.Y.: Simon and Schuster, Inc., 1975.

ALGEBRA

Ayers, Frank, Jr. *Theory and Problems of Modern Algebra.* New York, Schaums Outline Series, Schaum Publishing Co., 1965.

Johnson, Richard E., Johnson, Cheryl G. *Algebra, The Language of Mathematics.* Menlo Park, California: Addison-Wesley Publishing Co., Inc., 1975.

FINANCE

Ayers, Frank, Jr. *Theory and Problems of Mathematics of Finance.* New York: Schaum's Outline Series, Schaum Publishing Co., 1963.

Bowen, Earl K. *Mathematics with Applications in Management and Economics.* Homewood, Illinois, Richard D. Irwin, Inc., 1972.

Campbell, Colin D., Campbell, Rosemary G. *An Introduction to Money and Banking.* Hinsdale, Illinois: The Dryden Press, 1975.

Weston, J. Fred, Brigham, Eugene F. *Managerial Finance.*
Hinsdale, Illinois: The Dryden Press, 1975.

GEOMETRY AND TRIG

Jurgenson, Ray C., Maier, John E., Donnelly, Alfred J.
Modern Basic Geometry. Boston: Houghton Mifflin Co., 1976.

Wooton, William, Beckenbach, Edwin F., Buchanon, O. Lexton,
Jr., Dolciani, Mary P. *Modern Trigonometry.* Boston:
Houghton Mifflin Co., 1976.

SCIENCE

Chemical Education Material Study, *Chemistry, An Experimental
Science.* San Francisco: W. H. Freeman and Co., 1973.

Halliday, David. *Introductory Nuclear Physics.* New York:
John Wiley & Sons, Inc., 2d ed., 1962.

Physical Science Study Committee. *Physics.* Boston: D.C.
Heath and Co., 1970.

Physics for Students of Science and Engineering, Part II.
New York: John Wiley & Sons, Inc., 1960.

Project Physics Course. New York: Holt Rinehart, and Winston,
Inc., 1974.

Sisler, Harry H., Vanderwerf, Calvin A., Davidson, Arthur W.
General Chemistry, A Systematic Approach. New York: The
Macmillan Company, 2d ed., 1959.

STATISTICS

Kreyszig, Ervin. *Introductory Mathematical Statistics:
Principles and Methods.* New York: John Wiley & Sons,
Inc., 1970.

Weaver, Warren. *Lady Luck.* New York: Anchor Books,
Doubleday & Company, Inc., 1963.

Mosteller, Frederick, Rourke, Robert E., Thomas, George B.,
Jr. *Probability: A First Course.* Reading, MA.: Addison-
Wesley Publishing Co., 1970.

Spiegel, Murray R. *Theory and Problems of Statistics.* New
York: Schaums Outline Series, McGraw-Hill Book Company,
1961.

GENERAL

Adler, Irving. *Magic House of Numbers.* New York: The New
American Library of World Literature, Inc., 1957.

Burns, Marilyn. *The I Hate Mathematics! Book*. Boston: Little, Brown and Company, 1975.

The World Almanac & Book of Facts 1976. New York: Newspaper Enterprise Association, Inc., 1975.

Selby, Samuel M. *Standard Mathematical Tables*. Cleveland: 21st ed. The Chemical Rubber Co., 1973.

Wallechinsky, David, Wallace, Irving. *The People's Almanac*. Garden City, N.Y.: Doubleday & Company, Inc., 1975.

PUZZLES AND GAMES

Dudeney, Henry Ernest. *536 Puzzles & Curious Problems*. New York: Charles Scribner's Sons, 1967.

Judd, Wallace. *Games, Tricks, and Puzzles for a Hand Calculator*. Menlo Park, California: Dymax, 1974.

Judd, Wallace. *Games Calculators Play*. New York: Warner Books, Inc., 1975.

Rogers, James T. *The Calculating Book, Fun and Games with your Pocket Calculator*. New York: Random House, 1975.

Schlossberg, Edwin, Brockman, John. *The Pocket Calculator Gamebook*. New York: William Morrow and Company, Inc., 197

Thommen, George S. *Is This Your Day? How Biorhythm Helps You Determine Your Life Cycles*. New York: Crown Publishers, Inc., Rev. ed., 1973.

Vine, James. *Boggle, Calculator Word/Number Games*. Los Angeles: Price/Stern/Sloan, 1975.

Wylie, C.R., Jr. *101 Puzzles in Thought and Logic*. New York: Dover Publications, Inc., 1957.

Index

This *material* is supplied without representation or warranty of any kind.
Texas Instruments Incorporated therefore assumes no responsibility
and shall have no liability, consequential or otherwise of any kind
arising from the use of this *material* or any part thereof.